RURAL BANKING AND AGRICULTURAL FINANCE IN INDIA

Promise and Reality

Durgadas Roy

RAJAT PUBLICATIONS
Publishers & Distributors
NEW DELHI - 110 002

Rural Banking and Agricultural Finance in India

This edition is published by Rajat Publications
4740/23, Ansari Road Daryaganj,
New Delhi - 110002

ISBN: 978-81-7880-200-8

Edition 2026

Printed and bound in India

RAJAT
PUBLICATIONS

4740/23, Ansari Road, Daryaganj,
New Delhi- 110002 (India)
Tel:- +91-11-23267924
Mob:- +91-9811484973, +91-9811105389
E-mail: rajat_publication@yahoo.com

PREFACE

This book is the outcome of the research work done by the author as 'Emeritus Fellow'—University Grants Commission, Delhi during the Fellowship period (1998-2000). This book is based mainly on the Report submitted by the Fellow after the completion of the Research Work in 2001. I am grateful to the authorities of the University Grants Commission, Delhi for the financial support but for which the study would not have been possible. Many changes have occurred on the Indian Economic Scenario since the submission of the Report to the UGC. I have tried to incorporate all these changes in various chapters of the book. A new chapter has been added on 'Micro Finance in India' under the title : '*Micro Finance—The New Development Paradigm*'. This has added a new dimension to the quality and modern outlook of the book.

As for the materials and empirical data upon which this study has been based, major reliance has been placed upon official and non-official records, Annual Reports and Bulletins. Thanks to the Reserve Bank of India's cooperative research section, Agricultural Credit Department, NABARD and other credit institutions. The format of presentation chosen here has been found extremely well suited not only for students, academics and policy makers, but also people engaged or interested in business and finance. The book it is hoped, will be of interest to both the specialist and the laity.

This work is based upon the belief that serious effort and integrated forethought can contribute—indeed, are indispensable — to progress in the coming decade towards a more humane and practical, productive and self-sufficient economy. And it rests upon the hope that readers of this work whether or not they agree with my point of view—may be helped to think more informedly about the opportunities and the dangers that lie ahead and the consequences of various courses of future action.

—Durgadas Roy

Contents

1

Introduction and Overview

Rural banking has now become a subject of both practical importance and academic analysis in India. Usually, there is a wide gulf between those whose concern is the former and those whose mandate is the latter. This is unfortunate. The lack of inter-twining between theory and practice impoverishes both and retards the progress of society, towards which both efforts are dedicated. In the last two-and-a half decades the rural banking structure has been expanded spatially throughout the country. However, it has not been characterised by robust financial health and over the years the structure of rural banking itself has been viewed as an unviable one.

In the last few years rural banking and agricultural finance have become important economic and political issues. From the days of Indian banking confined largely to traditional sectors, especially trade and industry, the policy shift towards the rural banking, accelerated greatly since the nationalisation of fourteen commercial banks in 1969, has become an important factor dominating the growth of Indian banking. The reaction to these developments have been from excitement to despair depending upon the profile and the personality of individual commercial bank. Both these feelings have been evenly balanced today by the sizeable experience which has confirmed both the hopes as well as the fears. The time has therefore come to examine this experience in some depth and to review where we have gone right and why, and where we have gone wrong and because of what reason.

One of the major differences between the developed and the developing countries has been the failure of the latter to systematically throw up institutions, especially economic institutions, geared to the needs of the society. It is, therefore, a not-too-strange paradox that in India, a country which is eighty percent rural, where seventy percent of the population is engaged in farming and allied occupations, and fifty percent of whose national income is derived from agriculture, commercial banks until recently ignored the rural sector. There are of course a plethora of arguments—relying on history, technology and economy—in justification of this omission, and, were it not for the fact that these defensive reflexes at times continue to plague our policy thinking, they would hardly deserve and serious response in the present national context.

Unfortunately, there is as yet no conviction that Rural Banking is Indian Banking even amongst many policy makers. While equal access to education is enshrined in the constitution, equality of economic opportunities by way of banking facilities does not even gain acceptance as a long term goal, to be attained with all deliberate speed. Many important national decisions appear to be made with insufficient forethought and even less pre-planning. It is therefore all the more disturbing that even two decades after the well conceived enunciation of the New Banking Policy and the decisive nationalisation of the major banks, implementation of social objectives is viewed mainly as a patriotic duty, which, like standing at attention for the national anthem at the end of a cinema show, is to be fully carried out. Many of us just 'know' that:

(i) rural branches are a losing proposition,

(ii) agricultural finance is costly and risky,

(iii) lending to small borrowers is a humanitarian act which cannot really uplift the borrowers economically. Such honest beliefs, strongly held, are self-fulfilling prophecies, they will spell the doom of the entire experiment.

The success of social banking experiment of the Indian bank compelled the policy makers in the Government of India to give a new reading to the principles of banking, which ultimately has resulted in nationalising the major commercial banks. These nationalised banks were assigned the task of economic and social reconstruction of the country. But, unfortunately, as decades passed by, one bank after another started losing their grip over social banking operations. The losses started mounting up in almost all the banks. Suddenly, the entire balance for the degeneration of the banking sector was put on social banking. The conservative bankers, who have no social commitment whatsoever, branded rural banking as the villain of the banking disaster, and it was made to carry the cross of all the evils of banking sector.

But, the question is whether this is true? Are we objective in our criticisms against social banking? Umpteen number of research studies—which were undertaken by various social scientists and research institutions—show that the social lending has not been the primary cause for the problems of the banking sector. Social banking operates under a set of precondition. But after the nationalisation of the commercial banks the banking services has been impersonalised so much, that the natural rhythm of banking got disturbed. Extreme bureaucratization, politicisation particularly in the matters related to the appointment of the Chief Executives, for banks centralisation of policy making process, cynical attitude of some of the conservative bankers who disdain rural society, urban bias in recruitment, lack of social training for the bank staff, and various other administrative and procedural failures together destroyed the very spirit of social banking. In an inegalitarian society, the socio-political dilectics often tend to ignore the weaker sections, sectors and regions of the society. Banking is also not an exception to this dictum, Despite the low rate of delinquency in the case of priority sector advances when compared to that of industrial sector, the capitalist attitude turns all its guns unkindly against the advances to the core sectors and the less-privileged sections of the society.

It is well recognised in India to-day that some banks have been more effective than others in rural banking. In fact some pockets in each bank have been more successful than the others. On the other hand, some banks had been more aggressive in this direction in the past when they were smaller than they are today, there are lessons to be learned from each of these experiences and a constructive study of specific cases and conceptualisation of the successful strategies world amply repay the effort. Little has, however, been done in this regard and even today there is no effort to learn adequately, from the real life experiences where we have succeeded in reasonable measure, instead of trying to find out why we have succeeded, where we have, there is a great deal of emphasis on our failures, on areas where the achievement has been less than satisfactory. This is indeed, not conducive to either good policy formulation or to improving our practice.

It should be noted that the viability of any Unit of banking including rural banking is a function of generating sufficient spreads and margins to cover the transaction costs and the risk costs. However, the transaction costs itself is a function of volume of working funds. For a given amount of operating expenditure higher the volume of working funds, the lower the transaction costs and vice versa. The risk is a function of default rate or overdue rate. The lower the overdues lower will be the risk cost.

Non-viability is a result of non-performance rather than of the structural deficiency in the rural credit system. Institutions which are at present unviable have scope for turning around which is indeed viable. The possible solution which is indeed available to these institutions is the adjustment of their assets and liabilities proportions. The factors governing viability of rural banking operations are not totally out of control as there is no inherent in-built non-viability about these operations. A look at the steps to be taken by the banks and implementing them in a systematic manner would ensure the viability of these operations.

Basically the issue in rural banking is one of developing a strong banking presence. The most importance constituent of this is the opening of rural branches, is not a matter merely of locating a physical banking set-up, it has to perform in an environmental context and to develop opportunities for itself. From that point of view, what the rural branch can do with its given setting is by far the most crucial issue. Ultimately this itself depends upon what human resource the branch has and how that human resource is able to galvanise its own potential and that of its environment into an effective banking presence. In particular there has to be a systematic effort to participate in the development of rural sectors of the economy, especially agriculture in its various facets. Barring some bank branches which have had the good fortune of devoted professional leadership, this has not generally happened indicating the human limitations in the growth of rural banking.

The broader question is, what do we want rural branches to do? By far our main concern is with an effective deposit mobilisation programme, a well developed activity of financing agriculture, actually doing so and ensuring that as wide a group of borrowers is serviced as possible. In doing all this the commercial banks in India have faced several problems. Above all, their familiarity with rural areas has not been too good. Even more, the new financing sector like agriculture has been the *bete noire* of the Cooperative banking system besides being an area which is both complex and difficult to handle given the entire traditions of Indian banking.

Of no small consequence has been the problem that the people themselves in rural areas have been unused to the modern system of banking. For a long time a commercial bank in most parts of India has been a distant institution, an institution meant for the well-to-do urban elite, certainly an institution which was a little frightening experience with its aura and stern traditional character.

All these are complex enough issues for any developed system of banking anywhere in the world. Barring some of the socialist nations about whom we do not have adequate information, it is quite likely that there was no experience of such parallel in the developed countries of the West or of the developing regions of Africa, Asia and Latin America. The response of the Indian banks had therefore to be based on our own local, intuition, our will, and indeed our genious. It is premature to suggest that we have achieved major successes. If however, we were to take the best of our experience alone, we could perhaps say that if such an experience was converted into policy, we may very well achieve considerable success in the future. This would require a high level of skill in carefully converting the experience into policy and then monitoring performance systematically in the coming years. Several important steps have yet to be taken in this direction at the national and the industry level.

By far the most important role of the commercial banks through rural banking lies in its desire and the ability to promote development. This itself requires a great deal of familiarity with local rural issues and even more important a will to convert every potential economically viable proposition into the actual economic activity. It is indeed an entrepreneurship of high order which the banks have been called upon to perform. The task however, is not only for the commercial banks, even if the industry is able to sustain a rate of rural branch expansion of one thousand per year. From that point of view, the strengthening and revitalisation of the cooperative banking institution is a must and an effective linkage has to be worked out between the commercial banks and the cooperative banking system. This however can only be deliberately and systematically phased in an attempt to take banking to the last person in rural India. Towards this objective, the system of Farmers' Service Society as a Cooperative institution with effective linkage with Commercial banks is an important innovation. Basically the concept tries to marry the strength and the managerial capability of the commercial banking system with the spirit of the cooperative system. An important area that needs to be researched is the co-relation between the size and/or age of the bank, its entrenchment in the local area, and its effectiveness in rural banking. There is significant impressionistic evidence, both through cross-sectional and longitudinal observations that small and young banks show better performance in rural areas at less cost. If these observations can be supported by systematic studies, the policy ramifications of the evidence would have to be carefully considered.

While these would be important developments in the coming years, it deserves to be emphasised that banking institutions whether of commercial or cooperative vintage, cannot do everything for rural areas. While they can play a certain promotional—developmental role and equally important effective supportive financial role, there will be many sectors and areas which will been beyond the pale of banking institutions. The social infrastructure and other sociological inputs for instance will remain key to rural development and may have to be provided by the State. Perhaps new institutions may be necessary to be established by the State for such a purpose such as the area corporations. The banks however, could undertake to support and to develop economic activities which have potential or actual commercial viability. The important issues, here will remain as to the manner in which these two sets of activities are organised as well as interfaced. Perhaps the interfacing would have to be done by a far better system of multilevel planning and State leadership.

Since I am concerned with rural banking, I would like to say that good rural banking needs something more than specialised learning in various aspects of banking. Good rural banking needs good bank men who view their job as an opportunity to build up not simply a prosperous but a just and equitable rural society. Their training must acquaint them with the rural reality, the reality of abject poverty, injustice and exploitation of the weak and the down-trodden. The rural banker should have a proper perception of the sources and causes of this poverty, injustice and exploitation and in his limited capacity as a banker, should be concerned with their elimination. In brief, the training programme should go beyond imparting technical and specialised training and should try to inculcate a right attitude and motivation towards problems of rural banking. Though it is perhaps too much to expect, the banker should view his rural development assignment not simply as a part of his career but as an opportunity to fulfil some of his nobler urges. This view of the rural banker should also be reflected in the selection of the candidates. While their academic qualifications must get due weightage, the final selection should be determined by the candidate's aptitude and motivation for the type of service he is expected to render to his clients. I do not think there is a dearth of such young man in rural and semi-urban complexes. There are thousands of workers in voluntary agencies who are working in these areas with exemplary devotion, without expectations of high monetary benefits. The rural banking service provides opportunities for similar work with more resources and remuneration comparable with that received by government employees in the same location.

To sum up, my concept of rural banking is one of a conglomeration of a large number of small credit outlets, operating with a low-key establishment profile and low establishment costs. The client must feel at ease while entering its precincts and negotiating a loan. At the same time, the borrowers will have to be told that institutional banking has a discipline of its own, that there will have to be a scrutiny of the purpose of borrowing, the viability of the enterprise for which loan is proposed and it will have to be repaid according to a carefully derived schedule of repayment. The credit will be supervised to ensure that there is no diversion of funds and the enterprise is being managed efficiently.

2

Background and Perspective

Rural finance is primarily agricultural finance and a large part of this refers to the needs of the cultivators, as distinguished from processing and marketing of agricultural produce. Credit has sometimes been called the hand-maid of production and finance is a crucial part for the development of agriculture. Credit is required for purchase of inputs like fertilizers and seed, for payment of farm labour charges, and for meeting the domestic expenditure of the cultivator's family during the period between sowing and harvesting. This is called the production credit or working capital for cultivation. Credit is also required for replacement of wasting assets on the farm and also for new capital investment. This is called investment credit for long period operation. Credit is not only essential, it is indispensable. It is not necessary objectionable; nor is it a sign of weakness. The problem of building an effective rural credit structure adapted to this country's system of farming, government and institutional structure will not be answered by any new invention or desire imported from outside. The needs will have to be met in the hard way-by by giving unified and in some cases new direction to familiar institutions, making them work, filling them in, regrouping and reorganising them when necessary. And institutional credit is the major need of the day because it frees the cultivator from the clutches of moneylenders and enables him to obtain credit that is cheaper, systematised and productive.

No blueprint can be drafted for an organisation that will quickly and easily provide credit to the farmers of India in amounts that conform to their needs and on terms that fit their capacity to repay. Not only can credit remove a financial constraint, but it may accelerate the adoption of new technologies. Credit facilities are also an integral part of the process of commercialisation of the rural economy. However, no amount of credit, even at the most reasonable rates, can guarantee higher productivity or incomes among the rural poor. Success in this respect depends on many factors, including the availability of complementary inputs and serious, sound credit policies, well-managed institutions and appropriate delivery channels.

The goal has been clearly stated by the Planning Commission:

"It ... the credit structure of the country is to be fully geared to an increasing pace of economic activity in the rural areas, an intensive effort at integrating all the channels of credit for the common purpose is needed...For providing these facilities all the existing agencies, e.g., money lenders, Commercial banks, Co-operatives and the state have to be integrated and harnessed to a common purpose. Such a comprehensive approach is essential for ensuring the best use of all the available resources of the nation... At this stage we would only suggest that in the wider solution of the problem the integration of financial agencies would have to extend to all organisations – cooperatives, commercial and other which act as repositories and suppliers of credit.

The history of the agricultural development in all advanced countries shows that such an integrated system of credit laid the foundation for agricultural development and prosperity. Whether there should be a single agency dispensing all types of credit, or a separate agency for long-term or for long and medium term, what form this agency should take at the State level and whether State agencies need to be integrated in a central agency at the All-India level, and what part the Agricultural Credit Department of the Reserve Bank should play in this organisation, are matters which will have to be considered in the context of the wider issues referred to above" [First Five-Year Plan, G.O.I.]

No one is going to produce a satisfactorily—working, all-

India rural credit structure at one stroke. It will result from guided growth. There are many weakness to be overcome and many problems to be met in the process of that guided growth. In a national that is trying to do as much in so short a time as India, that can only be accomplished by the united, strong and steadfast effort of the forces commanded or supported by the Central Government and by the states. The first step to be taken is to organise strong central leadership for that effort.

Many questions need to be weighed and decided, and answers to many problems of organisation and action found in the process of evolving an integrated rural credit system that contains the necessary elements of strength, growth and self-help, and ties to its service the essential forces of the Central Government, the States, the Cooperative Organisations, and the Financial Community.

Credit is considered as covering all advances made with expectation of repayment. Advances made to cultivators so desperately poor that repayment is not reasonably to be expected, should be carefully guided and supervised. To the fullest extent possible, the borrower should be helped to use the advances for productive purposes which under normal conditions will increase the production and income enough to repay the loan and interest, with enough margin in addition to improve his economic position.

Rural credit in India is a vast, complex jigsaw puzzle. Many are at work on it, and in some of its areas coordination is showing results. The pieces are coming together. But leadership and organisation have not been brought to bear on the total task. The important immediate question is that how that effort is to be organised and guided. The first step to be taken should provide the centre in which policies and courses of action will be determined, and the task of coordination undertaken. It is essential to bring together and held in close teamwork the agencies which have an essential part to play if the programme is to produce what India needs and expects of its rural credit programme.

The problem is not merely one of encouraging the formation of Co-operative Credit Societies where there none, strengthening those now existing, and furnishing supplement credit for their members. The Reserve Bank of India is supplying able leadership for that phase, working with the State departments and Co-operative institutions, and with cooperative leaders of India. The institutionalised farm credit system for India should be conceived and developed in the context of the total rural programme of the country. The nerve centre might undertake: To determine in broad outline the comprehensive and integrated policy of agriculture credit to be evolved as early as possible, (extending) to all organisations— Cooperative, Commercial and other –which act as repositories and suppliers of credit. To coordinate the work of existing agencies toward the development of an institutional pattern which will give full play not only to Cooperatives, but to other broad forces enumerated by the Planning Commission. This includes giving direction to movements that will make possible and encourage greater participation in rural financing by various institutions of the country, and will seek to encourage productive use of the capital now controlled by private money leaders.

The present system of agricultural credit in India consists of two sectors, viz. the institutional and the non-institutional. The non-institutional sector consists mainly of the professional and agricultural money-lenders, landlords, traders, commission agents, and the farmers' relatives and friends. The institutional sector comprises co-operatives, commercial banks and the regional rural banks. In spite of the significant expansion of the institutional sector, non-institutional agencies still continue to play a dominant role, although these agencies charge higher rates of interest and follow unethical practices, they continue to dominate the scene because the farmers find it more expedient to resort to them rather than the agencies in the organised sector. The main reason for this is that their lending procedures are relatively simple and credit assistance timely. However, the share of the non-institutional sector in the total borrowings of farmers has recorded a decline from more than 95% in 1952 to 85% in 1961-62, 75% in 1971-72 and to about 65% at present.

Since in the present context we are more concerned with the institutional sector, a brief description of the evolution of this sector appears relevant.

Efforts to build up the institutional financing system for agriculture commenced with the adoption of the Co-operative Societies Act in 1904. However, during the first three decades of the century, the village money-lender was the main source of finance for farmers. Several enquiries and studies such as Sir Malcolm Darling's Report (1935) and the preliminary and statutory Reports of the Reserve Bank of India (1936 and 1937) emphasized the fact that almost the entire farm finance was supplied by money-lenders. Various measures for debt relief and control of money lending were tried; this covered statutory reduction of amounts due, fixation of maximum rates of interest on mortgages and the protection of the agriculturists' interest and the specified items of his property against legal proceedings.

The government made deliberate attempts to nurture the Co-operative movement, to institutionalise efforts to relieve farmers from the traditional burdens of debt and to promote thrift. Gradually they assumed a more positive role as compared with their earlier characteristics of organisation for defence against exploitation by money-lenders. There was not only a steady quantitative expansion in numbers but also a growing diversity in the functions assumed by co-operative societies. However, the credit societies continue to predominate in the Co-operative system. Till 1947, the general thinking was in favour of promoting multipurpose primary societies in rural areas. During the period 1947-56; Cooperatives were recognised as an instrument of planned economic action and the cooperative system was considered more suitable than the departmental agencies for dispensation of rural credit.

When the organisation and registration of primary agriculture credit societies was started in the country at the beginning of the country, it was not contemplated that they would federate themselves into central financing agencies. Some of the larger urban banks, however, assumed the position of, and acted as, central financing agencies. With the passing of the Co-operative Societies Act of 1912, Central Cooperative banks came to be set up. In some cases these banks served the bulk of the societies in a province and dealt with them either directly or through the medium of quaranteeing unions of societies. In other the Central banks served smaller areas such as a district or part of a district and when in need of funds had resource to one another or to a provincial co-operative bank.

The Committee on Co-operation in India, 1915 (Maclagan Committee) envisaged that the co-operative edifice in each province should ordinarily consist of primary societies financed and supervised by Central Co-operative banks, the latter covering an area not exceeding a district and serving 200-250 societies. At the provincial levels the Committee wanted in each of the major provinces, an Apex Bank, act as a balancing centre, forecast and arrange for the credit requirements and be the financial head of the Cooperative Credit Organisation for the whole province. In regard to the possibility of substituting the central banks by branches of provincial banks, the Committee observed as under:

> "It has not infrequently been suggested that where there is an apex or provincial bank, the central banks might with advantage be converted into branches of it. It is contended that the concentration of banking skill and experience and the aggregation of funds and accounts in one place would entail a saving in management and that central banks would then be regarded simply as machines for taking in and giving out money under the directions of the provincial board, and could be left in-charge of managers on comparatively low pay. There is some doubt, however, as to the possibility of carrying on the work through a low-paid local manager and there is also the consideration that such a change would involve the loss of a good deal of service now done gratuitously. Even if it be admitted that there will be an economy in management, there are still further objections to be considered...Our conclusion, therefore, is that although there is no reason why branches should not be established in preference to central banks in places where Unions have been developed, local correlations should always be well weighed before the step is taken, and we imagine that in most cases it will for sometime to be the cheaper and more efficient course to adhere to the system of independent central banks" (page 72).

Thus the Maclagan Committee on Cooperation examined

the movement and made many valuable suggestions in 1915 for improving it. The next period commenced with the passing of the Government of India Act of 1919, which made Cooperation a transferred provincial subject in charge of a Minister. The Act of 1912 has been replaced by Provincial Act in Bombay, Burma and Madras since 1925, 1927 and 1931 respectively. In the early part of the period, the number of societies was much increased. A recommendation which had a far-reaching effect upon the credit picture was that made in 1945 by the Agricultural Finance Sub-Committee headed by Prof. D.R. Gadgil, appointed by the Central Government on the recommendation of the Policy Committee on Agriculture, Forestry and Fisheries, to report on the ways by which 'indebtedness could be reduced and finance, both short-term and long-term, provided under efficient control for agricultural and animal husbandry operations.' That Committee recommended that the necessary process of debt adjustment for all solvent debtors should be accompanied by complete reconstruction of the financial structure. Specially, it proposed the setting up by the states of Agriculture Credit Corporations to make mortgage finance available and to supply the credit needs of all credit worthy borrowers. It would work preferably through Co-operative Societies of short term and intermediate loans to the smaller cultivators. The Committee provided in its recommendations that where the state government felt that the Co-operative financial agencies were sufficiently developed to undertake all the work proposed for the agricultural credit corporation, no separate corporation need be set up.

With independence, the National Government felt that, prior to agricultural reorganisation and development in a planned manner, it was necessary to undertake a thorough investigation of the problem of rural credit. A dynamic policy in the sphere of rural credit and cooperation was initiated by the Reserve Bank in 1951 following the recommendations of the Rural Banking Enquiry Committee (1950) and the Informal Conference on Rural Finance convened by the Reserve Bank in1951. The more important aspects of this policy related to various procedural changes enabling State Cooperative Banks to borrow more freely from the Reserve Bank and arranging for the preparation of interim report on the Co-operative Credit Movement in practically every State in India based on local studies by its officers and containing schemes for reorganisation, an important part of which was state partnership in Co-operative Financial Banks. The Rural Banking Enquiry Committee rightly observed,

> "In any scheme for the setting up of a sound and efficient system of agricultural finance, sufficient emphasis must be laid on the building of a sound structure of primary institution, whether co-operative credit society or a multipurpose society. The weaker link of the co-operative structure seems to be mainly in these institutions where it comes directly into contact with the rural people rather than in the superstructure and more thought and effort should be devoted to the development" (Report page 49).

After independence, people's welfare became the guiding principle of all activities of government. Planning was accepted on the basis to regulate and promote economic progress so as to augment production, increase employment potential and lay the foundations of a balanced economy. The First Five-Year Plan came into operation in 1950-51, in which 'Cooperation' was recognised as an 'instrument of planned economic action in democracy'. It was recognised that the Cooperative agency was better suited than the State for ensuring popularisation of credit for productive purposes. The Plan, therefore, set a target of providing Rs.1000 crore a year as short-term loans by the end of the Fourth-Year of the Plan and Rs. 25 crore a year as medium-term loans and Rs. 5 crore a year as long-term loans by the end of the Plan. The First Five Year Plan stressed the role of cooperatives as under,

> "The emphasis of the Plan is on augmenting agriculture production. In this sphere co-operation, has a very significant contribution to make. Co-operation can help to increase the effectiveness of extension work. Other services which a cultivator needs for efficient utilisation of his land can also be made available through Co-operative agencies. Such aids as seeds, fertilizer, and implements on which depends the profitable exploitation of the resources of the soil can be effectively placed at the disposal even of the small farmer by cooperative

societies. In fact, in the field of agriculture, Co-operatives comprise almost every activity that is connoted by the term agricultural organisation. It is the best medium for promoting a progressive agriculture. Major items of agricultural development, e.g., consolidation of holdings, soil conservation and provision of facilities as well as current needs such as protection of the crops from pests, diseases and animals can be most effectively served through co-operative organisation." (First Five-Year Plan—Government of India).

Just before the commencement of the Second Five-Year Plan came the Rural Credit Survey which gave a new dimension to the entire cooperative rural structure. The Report was published in 1954 and its recommendations were accepted by the Second Indian Cooperative Congress held at Patna in March 1955, and at the State Ministers' Conference held in Delhi in March-April 1955. The Planning Committee accepted the recommendations and under the Second Five-Year Plan (1956-61) Cooperative Development Schemes were drawn up in all States and the Agricultural Credit Department of the Reserve Bank of India came forward as a friend, philosopher and guide of the Cooperative movement in our country. The Survey revealed that co-operative credit, in spite of their existence for over 50 years, accounted for only 3.1 percent of the total borrowings of the cultivators. Its Report lies at the bottom of the policy, progress, and problems in this field over 40 years. The Survey showed that private individual credit agencies, such as money lenders, traders, relatives and landlords, provided about 93 percent of the total amount of rural credit. In fact, the money lenders supplied about 70 percent of the total amount of the borrowed funds. The most startling revealation of the Survey was that the major portion of the loans from co-operatives went to the bigger agriculturists while the medium and small cultivators, constituting about 75 percent of the total cultivators in the country, received only a tiny fraction. Regarding the long-term credit, the Planning Commission had pointed out that "a major part of the advances made hitherto by the Land Mortgage Banks were for repayment of old debts" (Planning Commission 1953, pp. 234).

The Survey further observed that agricultural credit, as supplied by different agencies, fell short of the right amount, was not of right type and by the criterian of need often failed to reach the right people. Rural credit must be directed principally towards improving productivity. It must meet the long, medium as well as short-term needs, It should be properly supervised. Besides it was felt that the mere extension of credit facilities would hardly better the lot of our such agriculturists without adequate and business like organisation of marketing co-operatives. The existing system of co-operative financing was also found to have been automatically biased in favour of the big and large cultivators. The Survey took great pains in tracing the failure of the Co-operative movement in India to fundamental underlying causes. It concluded that the movement never had any chance of strengthening itself in the unfavourable economic-cum-social climate obtaining in the country as the 'heritage of a colonial economy' which shifted the focus of organised private financial power to urban areas with a wholly urban-bias in its outlook. To quote from the Report,

> "The failure of cooperative credit is explicable in terms of the total impractability of any attempt to combine the very week in competition with the very strong and expect them by themselves to create conditions, firstly for their emancipation from the interests which oppose them, and secondly for their social and economic development in the context of the severe disadvantages historically imposed on them... The problem is not so much one of reorganisation of co-operative credit as of the creation of new conditions in which it can operate effectively and for the benefit of the weaker. The prevailing conditions cannot be transformed by the very persons who are oppressed and rendered weak by their existence. The forces of transformation have to be at least as powerful as those which are sought to be counteracted. Such forces can be generated not by co-operation alone but by operation in conjunction with the State... The problem of rural credit becomes inseparable from that of the organisation of the socio-economic structure of the Indian villages itself, in other words, paradoxical as it may sound, the problem of rural credit in India is not primarily one of rural credit.

rather it may be said to be one of the rural-minded credit." (The General Report—Abridged edition, pp. 128).

The All-India Rural Credit Survey Committee came to the conclusion that the institutional set-up in which co-operatives had to be organised in India was itself not favourable to the growth of co-operation. Co-operation in India was a "plant held in position with both hands by government since its roots refused to enter the soil." But more than the roots of co-operation, it was the tentacles of private agencies that had acquired a fair grip on rural India. The Survey, therefore, recommended more direct and more intimate association of the state with the Co-operative movement. The main recommendations of the All-India Rural Credit Survey were – (a) State partnership at all levels on equal terms and privileges, (b) Integrated Schemes of credit and marketing operation, (c) expansion of Co-operative Training and education both amongst officials and non-official co-operators, (d) Nationalisation of the Imperial Bank of India towards state association with commercial banking and giving it a rural bias and (e) State participation in the organisation of Public Warehouse for promotion of storage and warehousing on an all-India scale.

The Reserve Bank was assigned the crucial role of implementing the Scheme of Integrated Credit with a view to building up a sound co-operative credit structure which could provide timely credit to the agriculturists for the development of the agriculture. Thus, the role of the Reserve Bank was that of an active collaborator in the drawing up of the schemes of development, working in conjunction with the Government of India; the State Governments and the Co-operative Banks. The effect of the steps taken by the Reserve Bank in pursuance of the recommendations as well as other commitments set up subsequently was the transformation of the Bank's role from that of lender of last resort to that of an active agency not only for the promotion of a strong co-operative credit structure in different states of the country but also for enabling the co-operative agencies to take to larger share in the financing of agricultural credit through appropriate measures of reform and reorganisation.

In the structure of co-operative credit as prescribed by the Survey Report, there was to be a State Co-operative Bank, a

Central Land Mortgage Bank, and a State Co-operative Marketing Society at the apex level in each state. At the district level, there was to be a district Central Co-operative Bank of a branch of a State Apex Co-operative Bank, a primary land mortgage bank and a district marketing society. At the village level, there were to be large sized primary agriculture credit societies, primary land mortgage banks, gramin banks and primary marketing societies. The most basic part of the programme of co-operative development is that which relates to the reorganisation of the primary society, in particular the agricultural credit society. According to the Report,

> "It is our considered view that the formula 'one society to one village and one village to one society' has failed in India because its underlying assumptions have proved incorrect...For these reasons, we recommend that the future line of development of co-operative credit at the level of the village should be unhesitatingly in the direction of bigger societies covering large areas. In other words, primary agricultural credit societies should hereafter be established, so as to cover, according to local conditions, groups of villages with a reasonably large membership and a reasonably adequate share capital" (Report – Abridged pp. 233-34).

The Rural Credit Survey Committee had also stressed that in establishing co-operative societies, their viability should be taken into consideration. The Second Plan which followed the Report of the Rural Credit Survey Committee did not provide for the setting up of new small sized village societies or for sanctioning financial assistance to revitalise and strengthen existing village co-operatives. To sum up,

> "the place occupied by co-operative credit in the rural finance of the country is very insignificant. Organisationally and financially, there has, at the apex level, been considerable expansion in the recent past, even so, the central banks still remain weak and largely un co-ordinated, but the weakest link of all in a chain which is weak at almost all points is the primary co-operative credit society. It satisfies none of the requisites of either good co-operation or sound credit. Its failure to promote thrift and savings is followed at too great

a distance by its failure provide in the village system of credit which is at once adequate, prompt and productive." (The General Report –Abridged Edition – p. 91.)

In November 1958, the National Development Council in its resolution on co-operative policy also recommended that the responsibility and initiative for social and economic development at the village level should be placed fully on the village co-operative and the village Panchayat which were to be considered as the primary agencies for improving all aspects of rural life through the efforts of the people. The revised policy in 1960 envisaged that the primary societies at the village level will provide the economic interests of its members in accordance with the co-operative principles and seek to achieve this aim by activities in different directions. In other words, it was expected to be a multi-purpose organisation which will provide credit to its members, promote savings, supply farm requisites and domestic requirements, and arrange for the marketing of surplus farm produce. Multi-purpose Co-operative Societies become a reality on a national scale due to a variety of reasons. Too much emphasis was laid only on credit aspect, often to the neglect of other service functions. The multi-purpose societies were not backed by adequate skills as well as technical, extension and other supporting services. On the basis of the recommendations of the 'Committee on Taccavi's Loans and Co-operative Credit' (Chairman, Shri B.P. Patel-1961) Government of India declared that co-operatives were to be ultimately its sold institutional agency for providing agricultural credit. In order to enable them to take over the entire responsibility of providing agricultural credit. The programme of strengthening primary co-operatives was again emphasised.

In this context, Sir Malcolm Darling, in his Report on Co-operation in India, observed as follows,

"The Committee have certainly made out a strong case, on paper at least, for a large increase in the flow of agricultural credit, but I cannot forget Professor Carver's dictum that farmers who do not keep accurate accounts (and how many do this in India?) and who have not a keen sense of values should avoid use of credit like the plague...What guarantee

> is there that it will (Credit) go only to the Credit-Worthy or that the cultivator with more money to spend will be more punctual in repayment, more provident and less feckless?" (International Co-operative Alliance Review, June 1955.)

According to him, if there is no link between the Co-operative Department and the department dealing with Community Development, co-ordination between the two may be difficult to achieve. Sir Malcolm Darling, in his Report published in 1957, has referred in this context to undivided Punjab where the link was provided by a district committee with the head of the district as the Chairman, and with other district representatives of the Co-operative and other departments. Sir Malcolm Darling pointed out that this arrangement left departmental control over the field staff unaffected, and there was no need to draw a disputable line between administrative and technical subjects. Referring to the state intervention, Darling raised the basic question, "How will self – help and mutual help face with so much done for the members by government ?..... Are they not likely to wilt, or even be crushed under the weight of the proposed state structure. It is intended that government should gradually withdraw from partnership as societies become more competent to manage their own affairs, but, as India knows, it is never easy to pursuade those in authority that the time has come for withdrawal, still less easy to get employees to train others to take their place" (Darling – 1955).

But India had already accepted the centrally planned development strategy wherein, not just state participation, but, the state playing a major role was a key element. Naturally, the Reserve Bank of India and the Government of India accepted the recommendations of the Rural Credit Survey Committee (RSC). The State Bank of India was created by the nationalisation of the Imperial Bank of India and started functioning from July 1, 1995. The State Bank was assigned the task of opening 400 new branches in rural areas during the first five years of its existence. To enable the Reserve Bank to meet the obligations placed on it in pursuance of the recommendations made by the Committee, the Reserve Bank of India Act was amended in the year 1955 to provide for the establishment of two funds namely the National Agricultural

Credit (Long-term Operations) Fund and the National Agricultural Credit (Stabilization) Fund. The effect of the steps taken by the Bank in pursuance of the recommendations of this as other committees set up subsequently was the Transformation of the Bank's role from that of a lender of last resort to that of an active agency not only for the promotion of a strong co-operative credit structure in different states of the country but also for enabling the Co-operative agencies to take a larger share in the financing of agriculture credit, through appropriate measures of reform and reorganisation.

It is interesting to note here a few points from the Reserve Bank of India's General Review Report of the Rural Credit Follow-up Survey of 1956-57. The evidence collected by this Follow-up Survey seems to indicate the superiority of multi-village co-operative societies in the fields of organisation and finance. Generally speaking, the multi-village co-operatives possess financial resources adequate enough to enable them to maintain full-time Trained Secretaries and this very much facilitates organisation problems. Though1956-57 Follow-up Survey Report was in agreement with the new school's advocacy for bigger several village co-operations mainly on the ground of practical advantages, entertain high hopes on state participation. In regard to State partnership in share capita, it was discovered in course of Follow-up Survey that in most districts neither the targets fixed were achieved nor were the allotted funds properly utilised. As regards State partnership in management it was found that the steps taken by the Co-operative departments of State Governments were extremely inadequate. It is interesting to note here that in contrast to the Rural Credit Survey Committee' emphasis on institutional finance, Mr. Chester C. Davis (who was requested by the Planning Commission in early 1957 to enquire into the problems of rural credit in India) was of the opinion that personal finance was more important in the field of rural credit structure in India. Mr. Davis made no attempt for arranging a scheme to bring the money lenders within the orbit of a reoriented type of personal finance. On the other hands, he stressed more on the possibility of developing private and some informal institutions for dispensing personal finance.

"The scarcity of readily available capital for the institutional

> credit system is indicated in the estimates given earlier of the high proportion of the total amount of credit which has been supplied to borrowers by personal finance – from money lenders, farmer lenders, and relatives. A quick look at the Indian scene indicates that the co-operative societies are not increasing their financial resources materially except for modest growth at the state and central bank level, part of which is due to purchase of share capital by government in some of the states. There is an increasing dependence of the Reserve Bank to supply credit to supplement the working capital of the Co-operatives." (Report on Rural Credit in India – Chester C. Davis, p. 15).

A thorough integration of personal finance agencies with institutional credit agencies is vitally necessary for the reorganisation of rural credit structure in India.

In the Second Five-Year Plan, various proposals regarding rural credit generally followed the recommendations of the Rural Credit Survey Committee. The Second Plan emphasised that

> "economic development along democratic lines offers a vast field for the application of co-operation in its varying forms. Our socialistic pattern of society implies the creation of large number of decentralised units, both in agriculture and industry. These small Units can obtain the advantages of scale and organisations mainly by coming together. The character of economic development in India, with its emphasis on social change, therefore, provides a great deal of scope for the organisation of co-operative activity. The building up of a co-operative sector as a part of the scheme of planned development is thus one of the central aims of national policy" (Second Five-Year Plan, Gr. I.)

Darling was particularly invited by GOI "to review some recent developments in the field of cooperation with reference to programmes in the Second Five-Year Plan." We quote below some of the observations made by him in his introduction to his Report submitted in June 17, 1957.

"The Second Five-Year Plan involves the most spectacular

> effort contemplated in the field of agricultural co-operation... In short, co-operation is to be the vital principal of all rural development...It has long been my belief that co-operation is the only satisfactory means of securing the peasant's well-being in this complicated world. But if this faith is to be justified, nothing must be done to endanger the movement, particularly at the primary level, where it has its real being. Too much is at stake and too many millions affected. Accordingly, in considering the programme...and its relation to the movement as it is, it was necessary to consider whether so much could be done in so short a time without endangering it.
>
> I hope it is not inappropriate here to speak plainly about the co-operative credit movement, and to enquire into the reasons for its failure to live up to the high promise with which it was spread over India many years ago. There can be no question that it was spread from above, nor that it failed to take root as living, growing organisations in a majority of places where it was seeded. If evidence is needed, the Rural Credit Survey will supply it, present estimates are that cooperative credit societies of all kinds are the source of considerably less than 5 per cent of total borrowings by cultivators. Aside from the lack of a steadfast and co-ordinated programme by the Central and State Governments, the great weakness in the cooperative credit structure in India has been at its base, in the primary village society. If the weaknesses at top and bottom can be correlated, the intermediate State and Central Organisations should present no serious problems" (Planning Commission 1957, pp. 1-2.)

In 1962, the Reserve Bank of India undertook a resurvey called the All-India Rural Debt and Investment Survey, 1961-62, to assess changes since the RCS 1951-52. It pointed out that, over the 10 years, borrowings from the co-operatives had increased from 3.1 to 15.5 percent but that private moneylenders still predominated. So far as borrowings during the year 1961-62 showed that, compared to loans from other agencies, the Government loans were insignificant, forming only 2.6 per cent of the aggregate borrowings during the year. There was little change in the purposes of borrowings from the co-operatives and household expenditure continued to be the major purpose accounting for almost half of the total. The proportion of rural households in the country owing outstanding loans to 'agriculturist money lenders' was at 15 percent (which was the highest among the various credit agencies) followed by professional money lenders at 11 percent and 'Co-operatives' at 10 percent. Thus the dominant feature of the problem of rural indebtedness in India arises from the activities of the money lenders who can operate mainly by capitalising on the perpetual poverty of the peasants. Peasants take new loans either for paying interest on old loans or for securing ready cash for marriage and religious ceremonies. Since the funds are not generally borrowed for productive purposes, there is every change that the original amount will never be paid in full. This, coupled with the helpless position of the borrower because of the absence of the other alternative agencies, makes the interest rates exhorbitant. In this typical Indian situation, money lenders do not have an opportunity of amassing wealth mainly through the snow balling of compound interest charges. Indian money lenders, however, get innumerable pecuniary benefits from having acquired a thorough grip over the peasant's life; control over the marketing of his crops at a nominal prices; control over the land itself, and also control over the movement of the peasant.

The Third Five-Year Plan (1961-62 to 1965-66) stressed the importance of rigorous development of a large co-operative sector as an essential prerequisite of a society based on democracy and socialism. It was stated that,

> "Co-operation should become progressively principal basis of organisation in branches of economic life notably agriculture, minor irrigation, small industries and processing, marketing, distribution, rural electrification and the provision of essential amenities for local communities," (Third Five-Year Plan, GOI).

It proposed to set up the Agricultural Refinance Corporation later called the Agricultural Refinance and Development Corporation (ARDC). The Corporation was set up primarily as a refinancing agency providing medium-term and long-term credit to State Co-operative Banks, Central Land Development Banks and Scheduled Commercial Banks for financing reclamations and preparation of land, soil conservation, mechanised farming etc.

Alongside these big changes in the pattern of agricultural production and development, some major changes in the pattern of land holding and cultivation have also been noticed, which have a bearing on the demand for agricultural credit. The last 15 years had witnessed a certain degree of progress in land reforms, but this had not been either uniform or comprehensive. While it is not our purpose to examine all the related developments in any detail, there are two or three significant features to which we would refer. First, there had been a recent trend in the direction of an increase in the number of holdings, the total number of agricultural holdings increased by more than 4.5 million between the years 1953-54 and 1959-60. Secondly, the extent of owned area under operational holdings had tended to increase while that of the leased-in area had been slightly on the decline. Thirdly, while mixed tenancy is widespread, pure tenancy appears to be on the decline. For the country as a whole, about 18 percent of the area was under mixed tenancy while only 4.2 percent was under pure tenancy.

To sum up, certain recent tends provide a new context in which the requirements of agricultural credit have to be assessed and arrangements devised for meeting them. First, agriculture is becoming increasingly modernised and remunerative, and, over a large area, getting transformed from a way of living into a form of business. Second, this involves increasing use of, and hence more cash outlays on, improved seed, chemical fertilizer, pesticides and adoption of improved cultural practices, and in some areas, a united degree of mechanisation as reflected in the use of power tillers, tractors etc. Third, the base of agricultural production is being broadened and strengthened through investment in terms of outlays on digging of wells, installation and energization of pump sets, reclamation of land etc. Fourth, a large class of middle peasantry (including mixed tenant) is coming up which has benefited from land reforms and whose holdings are not too small from the point of view of effective adoption of the new practices and inputs. Fifth, the member of very small holders is on the increase who have not only problems derived from the current non-viability of their units of farming but also difficulties in regard to access to credit, supplies, etc. Sixth, the area of Indian agriculture in which most of the new signs of change and progress are in evidence is restricted to irrigated tracts which, though expanding gradually, form still only a small part of the cultivated area, and no real break through in technology has yet been achieved which can appreciably benefit the dry areas. It is, therefore, probable that the benefits of the new strategy and, a related to them, of various facilities, services and supplies, envisaged under the agriculture programmes, will go to those sections of the agricultural population who are well placed in terms of natural endowments such as good soil and water or institutional or economic advantages, viz., the medium and large farmers in the irrigated areas. This, in term, is bound to affect the direction in which credit will flow, unless suitable correctives are introduced which, among other things, ensure that the better placed cultivators contributed more out of their own resources and borrow less from institutional sources, in financing the outlays on their land.

The Informal Group on Institutional Arrangement for agricultural credit appointed by the Reserve Bank observed at the end of Third Five-Year Plan that only 68% of the villages in the State were covered by agricultural credit societies and of this 34% were covered by dormant societies. It observed,

> "The assessment of the credit-worthiness and need of the societies, the determination of the terms and conditions governing the loans provided to them and other technical aspects of agriculture credit are all such as to call for a close relationship between the lender and the rural borrower. This kind of personal contact, experience and local knowledge can be best found only in a body like the board of directors of the Central Co-operative Banks, who are able to appreciate better than any paid staff, the real problem arising from local conditions. Experiences in more than one state has shown that, from the point of view of fulfilling these various functions and providing leadership to the movement at the district level, the branches of an apex co-operative bank can only be poor substitutes for the district central co-operative banks

> and, in most cases, the former have been replaced by the latter'" (Report-page 54).

As the dispensation of agricultural credit is a fairly complicated and risk laden business, provision has to be made for cushions and reserves at different levels. In this connection, it may be mentioned that the three-tier pattern of the cooperative credit structure has been adopted and worked successfully in a country like Japan where also agriculture is characterised by small holdings.

Rural Credit Review Committee (1969)

In order to make a comprehensive review of the rural credit system for agriculture including processing, storage and marketing, in July 1966, the Reserve Bank of India appointed the All-India Rural Credit Review Committee (Chairman, Shri B. Venkatappiah). In its Report, submitted in 1969, that is 15 years after the Report of RCS Committee in 1954, admitted that the Integrated Scheme of Rural Credit envisaged by the RCS Committee (1959) with State participation at every level of the Co-operative structure, had not been pursued or implemented vigorously in all the states, that co-operatively backward states were still lagging behind, characteristically, the remedy suggested was to set up Agricultural Credit Corporations in these States. The reorganisation of rural credit in the Reserve Bank, involving the establishment of an agricultural credit Board; the setting up of a Small Farmers' Development Agency in each of number of selected districts throughout the country, the creation of a Rural Electrification Corporation which among other things, is to benefit undeveloped areas with an agricultural potential; the formulation of a more active and much bigger role of the Agricultural Refinance Corporation, along with the enlargement of its resources; and the adoption of various measures for ensuring the timely and adequate flow of credit for agriculture through Co-operative and Commercial Banks –these are among the highlights of the recommendations made by the All-India Rural Credit Review Committee. Some of these proposals—notably these concerning the small Farmers' Development Agency, the Rural Electrification Corporation and the Agricultural Refinance Corporation were included both in the Fourth Five-Year Plan and in the Central Budget for 1969-70.

The Committee came to the conclusion that the non-institutional sources still accounted for 81% of the total agricultural credit, frequently fell short of standards of timeliness, adequacy and dependability. The Co-operative system had remained relatively stagnant both in respect of coverage of credit, needs as well as borrowing members as a proportion to the total number of members. Generally, the Committee also noted that overdues were heavy, and were rising from year to year. The Committee also observed that a large number of Primary Agricultural Credit Societies were neither viable nor potentially viable, and therefore, could be regarded as inadequate and unsatisfactory agencies for disbursing of production credit. In spite of impressive quantitative growth at the All-India level, the co-operative credit system had made slower progress in several parts of the country such as Assam, Bihar, Jammu and Kashmir, Orissa and West Bengal. The co-operative structure has undergone various stages of growth/modification with active intervention, support and assistance from the government. The process was facilitated by periodical review of progress at expert level, revision of polities and procedures, legislative measures as well as financial, administrative and technical support. The Agricultural Credit Department of the Reserve Bank of India provides the strongest organisational infra-structural support to the co-operative system by way of supervision and guidance, besides providing the financial resources. Moreover, the Agricultural Refinance and Development Corporation play a vital role in helping co-operatives to expand their terms lending by way of assistance in project formulation, appraisal as well as refinance. In addition, the National Co-operative Development Corporation provides the basic infra-structure and stimulus for the promotion of marketing, processing and storage activities related to agricultural inputs and produce. Term credit for financing investment in agriculture received considerable emphasis in the Review Committee's Recommendations. The Committee suggested in respect of all such loans, that the technical feasibility and economic viability of the schemes should be regarded as a primary consideration. And it was in this connection with the term credit requirements for investment in agriculture that the Committee assigned a role of growing importance to the Agricultural Refinance Corporation.

Recognising the importance of the cooperative agency as an important means for bringing about the desired economic and social justice, the Planning Commission in its document on the Fourth Five-Year Plan (1969-74) had observed that, Co-operative banking and credit had played a significant role in the rural economy of a number of states: "Co-operative processing has contributed substantially to the growth of agro-industry in some states and the co-operative marketing structure has proved an important agency in implementing Government's food policy in recent years," The document had further observed that. "... it is important for planned development to bring about the growth of co-operation in all parts of the country and to ensure the co-ordinated operation of various types of Co-operative organisations." In regard to agricultural credit, in particular, the Planning Commission had indicated that co-operatives would continue to be the principal agency for agricultural credit, although other institutional agencies would have to supplement their efforts in the wider context of ensuring adequate credit for sustained agricultural growth. In short, agricultural co-operatives on the one hand and the consumers Co-operation on the other would occupy a central position in a strategy for co-operative development in the Fourth Five-Year Plan with the objective of institutionalising, to the extend possible, the services required by the farmers and the consumers" (Fourth Five-Year Plan Document: GOI.)

Taking an overall view of the entire agricultural credit situation, the Plan document had accepted the estimate of the All-India Rural Credit Review Committee (1969) of Rs. 2000 crore of short-term credit needs by 1973-74 and medium-term investment credit at Rs. 500 crore and long-term investment credit of Rs. 1,500 crore during the Plan period. It was against this background, the Plan document advocated a multi-agency approach, while emphasizing at the same time, the need for continued efforts for strengthening the co-operative agency. In regard to long-term credit, their advances would be the order of Rs. 700 crore during the Fourth Plan period, in addition to a sum of Rs. 200 crore that would be refinanced by the Agricultural Refinance Corporation. The Commercial banks which had entred the field of agricultural credit in a large way following nationalisation of major banks were also expected to increase their direct advances for agriculture to Rs. 400 crore by the end of the Fourth Plan period.

In view of the existing weakness of the institutional credit structures in the districts covered by SFDA/MFAL programme over the country as a whole, the National Commission on Agriculture in December 1971 in its Interim Report on "Credit service for Small and Marginal Farmers and Agricultural labourers" had suggested the setting up of multi-purpose Farmers' Service Societies to be linked to Commercial banks in SFDA and MFAL areas. The recommended integrated agricultural credit service has to take a two-tier formation with—

(a) Farmers' Service Society at the block or tahsil level, and

(b) Federal Union or Separate Functional Commodity Unions at the district level.

These organisations are to be co-operative enterprises with very clear and binding links with the Lead Banks. The main considerations for recommending this framework by the Commission were that there should be one single multi-purpose agency to serve the needs of small and marginal farmers, landless labourers, craftsman and village artisans as in the views of the Commission, the main handicap faced by these people had been their inability to contract separately a number of different agencies for different requirements.

The uniqueness of the farmers' service society lies in the total responsibility it assumes for agro/rural development and the requirements for the operations of all its members particularly small and marginal farmers and artisans at a single point. Another fact of its uniqueness lies in its attempt to utilise to the best advantage, the suitability of the co-operative form of organisation at the ground level, and blending it with the business acumen and experience of the commercial bank; the arrangement has the potential of enabling commercial banks to reach a large number of farmers as compared to the number they can possibly reach by directly financing individual farmers. The general relationship between the farmers' service societiy and the financing bank is that of a client and banker. The bank will not only be concerned with the profitability and safety of its lending to a farmers' service society in the narrow sense; it will have a direct say in the development of funds released to the farmers' service society to ensure the air safety and utilisation for the purpose for which they are intended. Besides laying down the basic procedures for lending, credit administration and repayment of loans, it will have the right to be continuously informed about the major financial transactions and decisions of the farmers' service society, and to advise the farmers' service society to play its growth on healthy lines.

To speed up the flow of institutional agricultural credit to the vulnerable sections of the rural community, the Government felt that it was necessary to establish "new institutions on the basis of attitudinal and operational ethos entirely different from those obtaining in the public sector banks" and set up a Working Group on Rural Banks (1975). The rationale behind the setting up of such banks consists in the fact that for several years, state policy in widening and intensifying the institutional coverage of rural credit laid emphasis on the development of Co-operative credit structure as the major instrument of building a viable rural credit scheme. In spite of significant progress made by the co-operatives, due to inadequate attention to the credit needs of the small and marginal farmers, the benefits have not percolated to all sections of farmers alike. And, in view of the relatively high-cost structure of commercial banks and inadequate local involvement, commercial banks lacked the ability to tackle the needs of the small marginal farmers, and agricultural labourers. Consequently, in accordance with the recommendations of the Committee on Rural Banks (Chairman; Shri M. Narasimham) necessity was felt for the establishment of an institution which combined the local feel and familiarity with rural problems and attitudinal identification with the rural economy, which the co-operatives possess in large degree, with the modern business organisation, commercial discipline, ability to mobilise resources and access to the central money markets which the commercial banks have." With their operational costs kept down to the minimum, regional rural banks are expected to make credit available to the small and marginal farmers at a reasonable cost. Their role is to supplement and not supplant the other institutional agencies in the field.

In the final report submitted in January 1976, the National Commission on Agriculture pointed out that the growth in the large overdues from year to year had affected the credit worthiness of the cooperative structure and also its ability to extend further credit to the marginal farmers and that the same was true of the agricultural lending by the commercial banks. Nevertheless, it changed the public sector banks and the co-operatives that they did not make any serious attempt to understand the special credit needs of the small bankers, let alone the marginal farmer or agricultural labourers. The NCA felt that, for this, a comprehensive grass-root level organisation was needed which would facilitate the conversion of credit into inputs and services as well as the realisation of fair price for the produce and would operate fully on commercial basis, covering all the needs of the small farmers (Ministry of Agriculture and Irrigation 1976, pp. 568-70).

The faster pace of growth in agriculture brought about by improvements in the technology of cultivation in recent years has given spurt to the needs of not only short-term credit but also capital investments on land by which alone improvements in agricultural technology can be introduced on a substantial basis. The Working Group appointed by the National Credit Council with a view to evolving appropriate organisational sector for implementing social objectives further observed that there were large institutional and credit gaps in the rural economy and underlined the need not only to mop up rural savings but also for the adoption of a multi-agency approach to meet the growing demands of rural agricultural credit.

It was against this background that the commercial banks were required to come in a big way to meet the production and investment credit needs of agriculture both through direct lending to farmers and also for other agricultural and allied purposes such as distribution of inputs and infra-structure requirements. And the experiment for bringing about inter-structural relationship between the urban-oriented commercial banks on the one hand and the rural-biased primary agricultural credit societies on the other was introduced as a step in this direction for supply of credit to fill in the gaps and promoting agricultural development. While even the combined resources of the co-operatives and the Commercial banks might be relatively inadequate to meet the demands of modern agriculture, it was obviously desirable that these two major financing institution should work in co-ordination with a view to avoid unhealthy competition, to ensure financial resources to worthwhile agricultural projects and to see that duplication and wastage of resources were avoided. It is also necessary to ensure that the co-operative institutions would not be weakened by the entry of commercial banks into this field, for the national policy is to promote and energising economic activities in rural areas.

Until the introduction of Social Control (1968) and Nationalisation of major commercial banks (1969), the official policy was to use the cooperative system as the best suited channel for institutional credit for agriculture. In fact, some efforts of commercial banks to go into agricultural financing were not looked with favour. However, with the introduction of social control measures and subsequent bank nationalisation, Commercial banks have made major strides in the financing of agriculture and emerged as an important source of agricultural finance alongwith the co-operatives. Agriculture in general is no longer considered a commercially unfeasible proposition. The Commercial Banks have experimented with a number of alternatives and combinations of methods and approach in different parts of the country, with varying degree of success. These include building up of a base of technically qualified field officers, developing expertise at head offices, group financing, adoption of villages, organising agriculture development branches, financing through primary co-operative societies and farmers' service societies on the lines suggested by the National Commission on Agriculture (NCA). For project formulation and consultancy services, the Agricultural Finance Corporation Limited was established on a consortium basis. Each district was allotted to one bank called the lead Bank' which would survey the resources and potential for banking development in that district, offer advice to small borrowers, particularly cultivators, assist other primary lending agencies, and maintained liaison with government and quasi-government agencies.

Thus the major role played by the Co-operative structure in the supply of agricultural credit lasted from 1951-52 to 1968-69 and there was a shift in emphasis from Co-operatives only to a multi-agency approach. This was both because of structural limitations of the co-operatives, which infact depended largely on RBI resources, and the failure of the co-operative sector to perform creditably its activities. Weaknesses in the movement continued despite all the efforts to reorganise and strengthen the co-operative credit institutions. Further, in November 1972, the Steering Committee of the All-India Debt and Investment Survey (1971-72), RBI, in its evaluation found that, although, the public sector banks did provide the necessary finance, they did not pay much attention to the revitalisation and reorientation of the societies and professionalisation of their management.

An earlier study made by the Programme Evaluation Organisation of the Planning Commission (1956-58) had revealed that the percentage of overdues to loans outstanding was between 31.2 and 46.4 per cent among large farmers and between 9.1 and 19.9 among small ones. Probably, the prevailing high interest rates in the free market provide an incentive for large farmers to borrow from co-operatives and other institutions and re-lend it to others. While the natural factors are beyond the control of financing institutions, the Study Team on overdues (1972) of Co-operative Credit Institutions had the following observations to make on willful default and on inappropriate lending policies and practices. "The cumulative effect of all the deficiencies in lending policies, especially inadequate and untimely credit or over-financing or lack of supervision over the end-use of credit, unrealistic due dates what is and, financing of defaulters had encouraged wilful worse default." (RBI 1974, p. 63.) Another most potent reason for wilful default in the last few years was political patronage to defaulting in the country. As regards the causes of overdues, the Study Team on Overdues (1974) had classified them as (a) external, i.e., those which are beyond the control of the lending institutions, like the occurrence of natural calamity, irrigation facilities and cropping patterns and (2) internal, to, those relating to organisational and supervisory arrangements obtaining within the institution. The Study Team's analysis shows that there has been lack of a direct and positive relationship between external factors and the level and trends of overdues. The general backwardness of a distinct or the occasional occurrence of natural calamity in an otherwise developed district only serves as a pretext for widespread wilful default. The conclusion appears inescapable that lack of will and indiscipline among the cultivators to repay is the principal factor contributing to the prevalence of overdues. Default thus appears to be by and large wilful, which at once makes it a problem to be tackled on the educational and social plane.

In the absence of an integration of the lending operations of the different institutional credit agencies, — Co-operatives, RRBs and commercial banks – multi-agency approach has given rise to a number of problems in an efficient disbursal of credit, this refers to the dangers of over-financing, under financing and multiple financing – leading to financial indiscipline and diversion of scarce resources for unproduction purposes. From the standpoint of lending agency, there are the problems of overlapping and duplication of banking facilities and consequent wasteful expenditure, besides unhealthy competition. With three different types of credit institutions viz. Co-operatives, Commercial banks and regional rural banks operating in the field of agricultural credit, problems of overlapping, varying interest rates on advances, etc., and consequent unhealthy repercussions have surfaced.

The Fifth Plan covered the period from April 1, 1974 to March 31, 1968. The Fifth Five-Year Plan should not be regarded as a big and ambitious plan. Its main defect was that it emphasised on too many items connected with urbanisation and industrial growth and did not possess that type of rural orientation which was required for dynamising agriculture and allied activities.

In March 1979, the RBI appointed a Committee to suggest improvements in the existing arrangements for institutional credit for agriculture and rural development (CRAFICARD). The Committee submitted its final report in March 1981. The National Bank for Agriculture and Rural Development (NABARD) came into existence on June 12, 1982 following the recommendations of the CRAFICARD. As it is inevitable, NABARD is patterned after the model recommended by CRAFICARD. The setting up of NABARD as an apex body for rural credit could be construed as a logical step in the organisational evolution of the Reserve Bank to decentralise its functions retaining the essential controls. The NABARD was to take over from the RBI the overseeing of the entire rural credit system including credit for rural artisans and village industries and the statutory inspection of co-operative banks and RRBs on an agency basis though the RBI could continue to retain its essential control.

NABARD since its inception in July 1982 has made significant strides in the field of rural credit. It had initiated a number of measures for angmenting the flow of credit to the rural sector in general and to small and marginal farmers, in particular, through strengthening the institutional rural credit structure. NABARD also decided to liberalise the terms of lending in order to stimulate credit flow to the rural non-farm sector. However, a close analysis of the flow of rural credit reveals that NABARD (including erstwhile ARDC) has met with little success in reducing imbalances in rural development. While Northern, Southern and Western regions accounted for two-thirds of cumulative disbursements the share of Eastern region comprising West Bengal, Orissa and Bihar has hardly shown any appreciable increase since mid-seventies.

The Sixth Five-Year Plan (1980-85) pointed out also that mounting overdues had clogged the system of co-operative credit. The rural leadership today complains that commercial banks do not handle effectively the whole complex of bank credit to meet the demands of the major part of the rural population. The low credit-worthiness of the poor comes in the way of the genuine needs being satisfied by banks. It should be understood that rural development is not just a development of the agriculture sector but an integrated development of a village covering agriculture, allied activities, village and cottage industries etc. In recognition of this, Ingtegrated Rural Development Programme was included in the Sixth Plan, as the most important and crucial programme for reduction in rural poverty and unemployment. It is true that the health of agriculture credit institutions, both co-operatives and commercial banks, was in a very sad state in many parts of the country. These possibilities were anticipated and articulated in the RCS Committee's Report (1954). But there appeared no straight-cut and easy solution. Hence, the conclusion, in the famous phrase, was, "Co-operation has failed, but Co-operation must succeed." (RBI 1954, Vol. II, p. 372.) The solution was to create "new conditions in which it can operate effectively and for the benefit of the weaker." According to the Committee's Report."... But if credit is sometimes 'fatal', it is often indispensable to the cultivator....Agricultural credit is a problem when it cannot be obtained, it is also a problem when it can be had but in such a form that on the whole it does more harm than good" (RBI 1954 vol. II, p. 151.) Unfortunately, this perception was not followed and a liberal credit was advocated not only where it was needed but where it could be taken. Without belittling the various efforts of the government and the banking and co-operative sector, it would be right to say that the endeavours made so far have not touched even the outer fringe of the rural population. It is high time that our financial institutions are used as social instruments for accelerated economic development and in the rural sector the objective can be achieved through agricultural finance and its optimal deployment for rural growth.

The non-institutional agencies have dominated agricultural finance before 1970's i.e., before nationalisation of major commercial banks in 1969. The main institutional and non-institutional agencies for providing agricultural credit and relative shares of different agencies in the total agricultural credit in India over three decades are presented in the following Table 2.1.

It is evident from Table 2.1 that the share of Institutional Agencies in the total agricultural credit increased from 7.3 per cent in 1951 to 63.2 per cent in 1981, showing an increase of more than eight and half times. It is also observed that the share of different institutional agencies increased considerably after nationalisation of Commercial Banks in 1969 (to be discussed later on) and establishment of Regional Rural Banks in 1975. The increase has been largely contributed by the Co-operatives and Commercial Banks including Regional Rural Banks. The increase in the share of other institutional agencies is only marginal, the relative decrease in the share of non-institutional agencies is mostly due to the decline in the share of moneylenders.

Table 2.1: Percentage Share of Different Financing Agencies in Agricultural Credit

(Percentage)

Credit Agency	*1951*	*1961*	*1971*	*1981*
A. Institutional Agencies (1-5)	7.3	18.4	31.7	63.21
1. Government	3.3	6.7	7.1	3.9
2. Co-operatives	3.1	11.4	7.1	3.9
3. Commercial	0.9	0.3	22.0	29.8
4. Insurance	-	-	2.4	0.4
5. Provident Fund	-	-	0.1	0.3
B. Non-Institutional Agencies (6-11)	92.7	81.6	68.3	36. 8
6. Professional money-lenders	49.8	13.8	13.1	7.8
7. Agricultural money-lenders	24.9	48.1	23.0	8.3
8. Relatives	14.2	5.2	13.1	8.7
9. Trades and Commercial Agents	0.5	7.1	8.4	3.1
10. Landlords	1.5	0.9	8.1	3.7
11. Other	1.8	6.5	2.6	5.2
Total (A+B)	100.00	100.00	100.00	100.00

Sources: 1. RBI, All-India Rural Credit Survey, Bombay 1951-52
2. RBI, All-India Rural Debt and Investment Survey 1961-62
3. RBI, All-India Rural Debt and Investment Survey 1971-72
4. RBI, All-India Rural Debt and Investment Survey 1981-82

Khusro Committee—Report of the Agricultural Review Committee

(Extract from the Summary of the Report of the Committee of the RBI – The paragraph numbers in bracket refer to the paragraph numbers in the Original Report.)

The problems of Indian rural financial market, the key messages of the Report, and suggestions for systematic improvements are briefly summarised here: In August 1986, the Reserve Bank of India appointed yet another Agricultural Review Committee

(Chairman A.M. Khusro) which submitted its Report in August 1989 (RBI 1989). The Review Committee seeks to bring out the views on the following basic questions relating to rural credit in India:

(1) What are the main basic problems confronting the institutional rural credit system in India?

(2) What are the root causes of these problems?

(3) Whether and to what extent these rural credit problems can be solved?

(4) How far the package of remedial measures recommended by the Committee help to rectify the situation?

The emerging agricultural technologies and the secular shifts in the agricultural sub-sectors in favour of commercially oriented agriculture are expected to create in the coming decades, a robust agricultural economy in India. It is to these changes and the associated problems that the rural credit system will have to effectively respond and gear itself [Paras –1.03 to 1.06]. Judging from the steep increase in the quantum of institutional rural credit over the last two decades and its coverage of rural population this object of policy makers can be said to have been by and large achieved although the credit pattern that emerged in the process is more skewed in favour of larger and small farmers to the neglect of medium ones. The future thrust has, therefore, to be on reserving the vitality of the credit structures which have shown signs of atrophy in the very process of quantitative expansion. There is no need for a major structural reorganisation as the basic foundations of the credit systems have been found sound and well suited to Indian conditions. [Paras – 1.42 to 1.45].

According to the Committee, many of the major ills of the rural credit institutions have arisen on account of over administered rural banking system. If the credit system is to play an efficient and effective role in future when the direct demand for agricultural credit will rise to Rs. 1,10,183 crores by 1999-2000 as against Rs. 27,551 Crore in 1989-90, it has to move "out of the stage of administrative paternalism, with rigid rules and stipulations, a plethora of interest rates for lending and borrowing and sprawling subsidies and other fixations", and "must come to be operated on much freer commercial and developmental lines." [p. 4.]

The Committee desires the rural banking system to be market-based and at the same time it should "assist vigorously in lifting the backward or less developed sectors like agriculture as also lifting the poor from the poverty zone to above-poverty levels and to do so speedily and effectively" [p4]. "The surplus generated in the economy as well as in the credit system from the efficient operation of the larger category should go to meet some of the costs and, if and to the extent necessary, some specific subsidies for the low income category" [p.5]. Though the expert group is in favour of freeing the rural banks from the shackles of administrative rates of interest subject to the present ceiling of 15.5 percent for agricultural lending, it has, however, emphasized the compelling need for a concessionary interest rate for the weaker sections, adding that "so long as the overall credit economy is generating surpluses, concessional rates focussed on the poor cannot do institutional harm but may do a great deal of social and economic good" [p.8].

The multi-agency system for rural financing was introduced with the avowed objective of (1) providing at least one alternative source of institutional credit other than the co-operative credit agency, particularly to ensure that the credit needs of the weaker sections in the rural areas are met and (2) bringing about healthy competition among the lending institutions which in turn benefits all the rural borrowers.

The vitality of the rural financial institutions depends on the vitality of the economy and the activities pursued by the borrowers. Recognising this inter-linkage, a better co-ordination between development planning and credit planning through a graduation of the present 'service area scheme' into a more comprehensive 'development area scheme' is necessary. The existing 'multi-agency approach' should be sharpened where CBs and Co-operatives supplement and support each other. Relative freeing of interest rates, a new and greater thrust on deposit mobilisation, more effective lending and recovery, etc., as recommended are meant to make the credit system more responsive to the emerging developmental needs [Paras 1.50 to 1.52]

All these could be achieved only if there is greater autonomy to the credit institutions. The growing inroads into the commercial banking system through excessive directions and controls and interference with the democratic management of co-operatives which debilitated these systems over the years are disturbing trends. There is need to reverse this trend [Paras1.85 to1.87]. The rural credit problems in the Indian context could be summed up as "credit well delivered will be well accepted—credit can be well delivered only by well conceived institutions." Indian agriculture will experience larger growth by the term of the century. It can also be expected to be a scene of relative sub-sectoral shift. This will need agricultural development programmes in different states being strongly supported by financial institutions to make agricultural and rural economies more viable, productive, progressive and profitable [Para 2.117].

As the Committee points out that, the place of the Commercial Banks in the rural credit structure rests on the fact that, if lendings to rural and weaker sections are to be at concessional rates, there has to be some cross-subsidisation and, in the Indian context, only commercial banks have the capacity to do it. (RBI, 1989, para 3.59.) But too much burden has been placed on the commercial banks. The commercial banks are inducted to achieve certain targets and sub-targets under priority sector lendings. Forty percent of the total credit is thus required to be channelled to identified priority sectors such as agriculture, small scale industry, small business etc. Direct finance to agriculture and allied activities is to reach a level of 17 percent of net bank credit and credit for weaker sections 10 percent. All these targets were achieved by the banks by March 1988 [paras 3.07 and 3.09]. The share of commercial banks in Integrated Rural Development Programme (IRDP) loans has gone up to 69 percent, compared to 23 percent that of R&Bs and 8 percent that of Co-operatives [Para 3.18].

The commercial banks have found sanctioning and monitoring of large number of small advances in their rural branches, time consuming and manpower intensive and consequently a high cost proposition. Partly because of this the banks have been found reluctant in posting sufficient supervisory and other staff in rural broaches. Consequently, supervision of rural advances has come to be neglected. Also the staff in rural branches of commercial banks lack sufficient motivation to work in rural areas for various reasons. If commercial banks are to expand in the rural areas, they should have the right staff, properly trained and motivated to man these rural branches. Incentives both monetary and non-monetary are necessary for these staff [Paras 3.34 to 3.37].

The overall recovery of commercial banks in respect of their direct advances to agriculture as at the end of June 1987 was 57.4 percent. Their recovery under IRDP was relatively less at 45.3 percent. There has, however, been variations in the recovery State-wise and bank-wise. Whenever Commercial Banks geared up their organisational structure, adopted schematic lending, improved pre-lending appraisal of schemes and launched recovery drives, the recoveries have improved [Para 3.38].

Under the Lead Bank Scheme started in 1989, the Lead Bank was mainly intended to act as a consortium leader for co-ordinating the efforts of all credit institutions in the allotted districts for branch expansion and for meeting the credit needs of the rural economy. The various machineries created under Lead Bank Scheme have, no doubt, created an awareness for better understanding of the problems at the ground level. However, many of these committees under the LBS have tended to become more ritualistic than functional [Para 3.39].

The overall profitability of the commercial banks has been under strain for sometime due to rise in the cost of deposits, declining yield on advances, rise in establishment expenses, etc. However, in recent years there has been some improvements in the absolute net profits of commercial banks. Losses on account of rural business of Commercial Banks have been contributing to their overall losses. Low interest rates on agricultural advances, lending under IRDP, relatively poor deposit mobilisation in rural branches, lower staff productivity, etc, have contributed to the poor profitability of rural business. As rural lending has been found contributory to losses compared with the rest of the business necessitating cross-subsidisation, commercial banks have been rather reluctant to expand their rural business and post further staff to support these lendings (Paras 3.52 to 3.59.)

Initially Commercial banks were rather hesitant to enter the field of rural finance but today they have forged ahead of Co-operatives in extending rural credit. One of the problems of such rapid expansion has been the deterioration in the quality of scheme preparation, particularly under the anti-poverty programmes. Such deterioration in the quality of lending was also due to heavy work-load of day-to-day housekeeping, without commensurate increase in the supporting staff. Over-dependence on standard norms without adequate flexibility in individual cases, under provision of production finance in support of investment finance, fixation of shorter repayment schedules than what is warranted, lending under poverty alleviation programmes without assessing the realistic potentials, etc., were certain other deficiencies in their rural lending. There was a tendency to rely more on walk-in-business or sponsored loan applications by the branch managers. Too many detailed instructions on several aspects of rural lending have led to a decline in the professionalism of rural branch managers. It is necessary to give them sufficient discretion so that credit decisions are taken within the overall framework of guidelines and for which they can be made accountable (Paras 3.66 to 3.80.)

The Committee concludes that if commercial banks are to emerge as a strong system to be able to survey credit effectively and efficiently in the rural areas, the targets for financing weaker sections and the rural poor should be reasonable, such as the system can bear (Paras 3.81 to 3.83.)

Coming to RRBs, the Committee points out that, in setting up the RRBs in 1975, the intention was to create an institution which combined the local feel and familiarity with the rural problems which the Co-operatives possessed and the degree of business organisation and modernised outlook which the commercial banks had. Partnered by the G.O.I., State Government and sponsor bank in the equity ratio 50,15;35, these new banks were conceived as low cost district banks exclusively to meet the credit needs of the target group, i.e., small and marginal farmers, agricultural labourers, artisans and other rural residents of small means [Paras 4.01 to 4.09]. But the local feel thought to be brought in by RRBs was 49 percent of demand, recovery of dues in respect of 81 RRBs was 50 percent or less of the demand. Wilful defaults, misuse of loans, lack of follow-up, wrong identification of borrowers, extension of benami loans, staff agitations, etc, contributed to the poor recovery in the RRBs [Paras 4.21 to 4.22]. The major factors which had contributed to the erosion of RRBs profitability were their lendings exclusively to weaker sections, low interest rate margins and high operating cost involved in handling small loans with no scope for cross-subsidisation [Paras 4.18 to 4.20].

In the present Committee's view, the objective of service to the poor could be achieved only by self-sustaining credit institutions. "RRBs, structured as they are, in our view, are not the institutions which could fulfil this function" [P144]. The Committee findings have brought out clearly that the basic advantages-supplementary rather than supplementing the existing institutions, low cost of operations, local feel through locally recruited staff, better absorptive capacity for refinance compared with Co-operatives—which the Narasimham Committee assured about the RRBs in 1975 has not been realised. A part of the reason for the failure of RRBs is on account of external factors such as socio-political environment. After examining various alternatives to strengthen the RRBs for enabling them to serve the rural poor more effectively, the expert group "found these alternatives to be unsatisfactory half-way houses which do not solve the problem of service to the rural poor" and concluded that there is "no place for RRBs in the country's rural credit system for the future" and they should be merged with the sponsor banks" [Paras 4.34 to 4.37].

The merger of RRBs with commercial banks will offer a solution to the problem of insolvency and the in-built non-viability of the majority of RRBs. The merger would also solve the problem of accumulated losses of the RRBs. Further, by providing the structural arrangement, it will have a built-in-self-strengthening and internal cross-subsidisation capability and would remove the innate weaknesses of RRBs. The emerging system will be able to achieve the goal of creating a strong viable credit system in which the interests of the small man would be better served [Para 4.54].

The streamlining of public sector banks is relatively easy as they are bureaucratic commercial institutions whereas the co-operatives are democratic institutions and, as such, pose many problems and hurdles in restructuring that set up. Further, while non-credit co-operatives are left on their own, the credit structure has more or less become another government wing. It should also be noted that while we have shown our competence in running efficiently higher level institutions, we have not been successful in streamlining the grassroots level rural credit set up both in the co-operative and commercial banking sectors. As a result of various efforts made following the Rural Credit Survey Committee Report in 1954, there has been improvement in the structure of co-operative system but the overall quality of co-operative character and operational efficiency deteriorated owing to "the politicalisation, officialisation, mass supersessions, low margins and lack of professionalisation in the managerial infrastructure at all levels as an inevitable consequence of excessive officialisation" [P. 184-85].

The Khusro Committee had taken a line, when it observed that paradoxically, state partnership in stead of strengthening the credit system has passed the way for ever-increasing state control over co-operatives, culminating in virtually depriving the co-operatives of their vitality as well as democratic and autonomous character. The net outcome of the above factor has been to impart a great deal of inefficiency, high costs, low or negative profitability, inefficient service and non-self reliance in the co-operative organisations especially at the level of PACs. "It is thus necessary that the county captures the spirit of co-operation, its culture, its discipline and above all its ethos. This can only be achieved with a cohesive structure based on a strong foundation at the primary level deriving inspiration from the higher ties which are professionally managed under a dynamic and motivated leadership" [Para 5.47]. So far as the co-operatives are concerned, politicisation of co-operatives takes place as a result of capture of management through the election process or wholesale supersession of elected boards by the State Governments. The Khusro Committee has stressed the urgent need to arrest the growing trend towards the progressive infringement of the authority of the credit system at all levels.

The Committee confirms that a major weakness of the co-operative system has been the neglect of the base level institutions and the tendency of the higher level institutions to look after their own interests often at the cost of the primaries. The co-operative credit system has woefully neglected its basic responsibility towards mobilising deposits, with the lower tiers looking up to the higher tiers for refinance at all levels [Para 5.22]. The essence or basic features of co-operative banking system must be a larger reliance on resources mobilised locally and a lesser dependence on higher credit institutions. Heavy dependence of outside funds has, on the one hand, made the members less vigilant, not treating these funds as their own, and on the other led to greater outside interference and control. Overall, this has made the co-operatives a mediocre, inefficient and state system. [Paras 5.7 to 5.29]. This is of course true, but while reiterating it, the committee completely forgets its own revelation, namely, that the vitality of the rural structure depends on the vitality of the economy, and the activities pursued by the borrowers. The fact is that agricultural credit co-operatives are essentially Co-operatives of the borrowers and there is hardly any scope for raising resources except by coercive procedures.

It has been said of co-operation that it has failed in India because it has been both state sponsored and State patronised. With the excessive government intervention in the affairs of the co-operatives, effective non-official leadership alongwith democratic management disappeared altogether [Para 5.15]. The powers which rest in the government under the Co-operative law and rules are all-purvasive. Compounded further by their lack of self-reliance and their dependence on high tiers and the government, the State has come to gain almost total financial and administrative control over the co-operatives, in the process stifling their growth. This trend must be reversed. Progressively, the powers, which lie with the Registrar today should be vested in the higher tier organisations in respect of its lower tier [Paras 5.36 to 5.38]. According to the Committee only a National Apex Co-operative Bank could fill the systematic gap and hopefully help to build the systematic strength and cohesiveness which stems from a Union of the State apexes. Hence, the Committee recommended the establishment of a National Cooperative Bank of India [NCBI].

Though the Committee as a whole has left NABARD untouched while recommending a separate national bank for the cooperative sector and considers that the new bank "will be of great assistance to NABARD in its vital role of institution building in the co-operative sector" [p. 333}, there is lurking fear regarding (i) the overlap in some respects between NABARD and the new bank, (ii) to what extent the co-operative bodies would like to delink themselves from the public sector banks, and (iii) about the real scope from the success of such a bank, particularly when it is expected to "function on its own momentum distancing itself from the government patronate with the concomitant government control and interference as well as props including support from it" [P. 336].

The National Bank for Agriculture and Rural Development (NABARD) came into existence on June 12, 1982 following the recommendations of the Committee to Review Arrangements for Institutional Credit for Agriculture and Rural Development (CRAFTCARD). The NABARD was visualised as a centre-piece for the entire rural credit system at the national level and as a provider of supplemental funding to rural credit institutions. The institution operates within the policy framework of RBI and GOI. Apart from providing financial assistance to NABARD, RBI has continued to maintain close links with it [Paras 9001 to 9.003].

The Committee has pointed out:

(i) NABARD's functions are an amalgam of activities inherited from the parent organisations rather than those of a unified apex institution.

(ii) The refinance function has attracted relatively more attention and resources over the years.

(iii) In future, NABARD should give greater attention to (a) leadership role in institution building specially to revitalise the Co-operative system and (b) non-farm business and agro-processing activities.

NABARD since its inception has made significant strides in the field of rural credit. It has laid greater emphasis on agriculture credit and, as a result, its assistance to agriculture and allied activities has gone up from the level of Rs. 703 Crore in 1982-83 to Rs. 1056 Crore in 1984-85. The drawal of funds from NABARD by RRBs has significantly gone up. NABARD has also provided substantial refinance from IRDP. The involvement of the NABARD in rural poverty eradication programme is amply evidenced by several measures initiated by it for the implementation of several points of New 20-Point programme.

If NABARD has to emerge as a strong development bank for rural re-generation, it has to take certain fresh initiatives. It should concentrate more on the building up of the co-operatives, improve its functional capabilities in project identification, for preparation, appraisal and monitoring, forge a better linkage between inspection and development function, pay greater attention to the non-farm sector and staff training and extend its net-work to the district level. NABARD will have to play its part in open market borrowing also, so that it could meet its refinance commitments. The present lack of control over its member institutions should be rectified by developing necessary clout with the help of and in co-ordination with RBI. In course of time, however, NABARD will have to evolve its own image to enforce the required discipline among member banks [Paras 9.125 to 9.127].

The rural banker henceforth is to be judged "by how much he succeeded in changing the economy of the customer and socio-economic face of the region," No doubt all this is desirable, but where are the ground level conditions to achieve the ideal approach involving a good deal of spade work and co-ordination? More ambitions approach only creates frustration and endangers even the simpler approach. Sometime back, B. Venkatappiah, the doyen among the experts on rural credit said that we have rural banks but not rural bankers. This raises the question about the suitability, skills, training and motivation besides the adequacy of staff working in the rural credit agencies. It is in this context we have to see what steps the expert group has suggested for improving the present unsatisfactory situation. According to the Group, a rural banker, "has to have not only the knowledge of banking per se, banking laws and practices but also various other skills. For instance, he has to have the right approach, attitudes and a style of management which is conducive to the genius and eithos of rural areas. He should have the knowledge of banking. He should also have the ability to assess the economic potential of the area in terms of the activities which offer scope for developing banks lending business. Effective communication ability is another quality which a rural banker has to possess so that he could deal with the rural clientele and earn their confidence" [P. 489].

In another words, he cannot be an ordinary conventional banker. One can imagine how strong the motivation and how intensive the training has to be if he is to be a rural banker. In this connection, the committee has made a significant observation. It has said that, "one lesson which emerges from experience in agricultural banking is that policies have often marched ahead of organisation and organisation, ahead of personnel...the problems of commercial banks in the development of banking in the rural lending one low motivation as well as gaps both in the knowledge and skills. Above all, the low level of sympathy for the disadvantaged classes and over-shadowing all these, the bureaucratic approach are other causes" [P. 490-91].

The problem of overdues has become extremely serious over the years due to various reasons including poor quality of loaning and political pressures. As at the end of June 1986, rural overdues of all credit institutions formed 42 percent of the total demand.

A comprehensive and critical analysis of the overdues syndrome based on field level findings is presented in the report. Such a detailed examination of the problem had not been attempted since the time of the Datey Committee in 1974. While discussing the overdues problem and supervision over credit, the Committee has said that, "organisational innovations like formation of self-help groups to act as links between credit agencies and borrowers" would also help in educating the farmers. The Committee has also commended the practice of giving loans on a group-basis. But it does not seem to have taken any stand on the functional societies in this aspect.

The economy entered the Seventh Plan (1985-90) period in a strong position because of the good work done during the Sixth Plan period. The rate of growth of GDP had accelerated over the past decade and the Sixth Plan growth target of 5.2 percent was fully achieved. Agricultural performance was particularly impressive. A major policy objective in the sphere of agriculture credit during the Seventh Plan period would be to ensure a substantial increase in the flow of credit, particularly for the weaker sections of the population, for the less developed areas especially in North-Eastern region, for dry land farming and for pulses and oil seeds development. Attention would have to be given to credit planning and monitoring in a co-ordinated manner at the National, State and District levels. The Plan document says, "The major thrust during the Seventh Plan period would be to ensure adequate flow to the weaker sections of the population to the less developed areas. The Planning Commission believes that for this purpose radical changes are required in the procedures and operational formalities followed for sanction and disbursement of credit. It is emphasized that during the Seventh Plan period, all efforts would be made to provide co-operative credit for production, investment and consumption through a single window. To give effect to the one window approach, the short-term credit structure would also provide investment credit and similarly the long term credit structure would also provide production credit." In fact, the "one window" approach serves as the kingpin for remodelling the Co-operative Credit institutions during the Eighth Plan period.

But the financial resource constraint and the balance of payments problem on top, of the unemployment bogey and the accute inflationary pressure plunged the Indian economy into a deep crisis when the Seventh Plan came to an end. As a result, there was a near halting of the planning process for two years [1990-91 and 1991-92]. In June 1991, the new Government of India announced a New Economic policy effecting drastic changes designed to correct the macro-economic imbalance and effect structural adjustment so as to bring about a more competitive system and promote efficiency in the real sectors of the economy. The country was passing through an unprecedented economic crisis and since mid 1991 a series of measures, including the devaluation of the rupee in July 1991, were taken to face the crisis. Sweeping reforms like trade liberalization, industrial decontrol and measures to attract foreign investment have been introduced. These are indeed far-reaching structural reforms which mark a complete departure from the basic approach to, and philosophy of, planning for development which we had adopted since 1951. These are not ad hoc measures but form part of the structural adjustment programme which is embodied in the memorandum on Economic Policies submitted to the IMF in August 1991.

Financial Sector Reform: and The Narasimham Committee

The structural reforms in the real sectors of the economy would yield optimal results if they are accompanied by a parallel reform of the financial sector designed to enhance the efficiency of financial intermediation. In this sense, financial sector reform is a necessary concommitant of trade and industrial liberalization policy. The Government of India therefore appointed in August 1991 "a High Level Committee to examine all aspects relating to the structure, organisation, functions and procedures of the financial system." The Committee, headed by M. Narasimham, a former governor of Reserve Bank of India, submitted its report in November 1991. The main strand of philosophy which runs through its major recommendations is summed up by the committee itself in the following sentence: "An efficient and market-oriented financial system could thus be regarded as a complement to market based decision-making in the real sector." "The Committee's approach to the issue of financial sector reform is to ensure that the financial services industry operates on the basis of operational flexibility and functional autonomy with a view to enhancing efficiency, productivity and profitability. A vibrant and competitive financial system is also necessary to sustain the ongoing reform in the structural aspects of the real economy." [Report of the Committee on the Financial System-Summary – Para 1].

The Report of the Committee could be said to be directed at Indianisation of the basic changes taking place elsewhere in the world, particularly in those areas which sought help from IMF and World Bank. Therefore, for a proper appreciation of the changes, we have also to take note of the global trends and changes in banking industry as a whole. However, the words of change were blowing in India even before the publication of the Narasimham Committee Report. The Ghose Committee Report on new formats for balance-sheet and profit and loss statement for commercial banks (1985), the Sukhamoy Chakravarty Committee Report on Monetary System (1985), the Vaghul Committee Report on Money Market (1987), the establishment of Discount and Finance House of India (1988), the series of Two Year Action Plan started in 1985 to improve the operational and structural efficiency and financial viability of public sector commercial banks etc, are the great land marks in the process of change. All these developments were largely at the initiative of the RBI which had only limited freedom to introduce effective changes in the financial sector. The crisis of 1990-91 hastened the process of change as it became necessary for the Government of India, which is the major stake holder in different sectors including the financial sector.

For analysing the implications of the committee's recommendations, these could broadly be divided into three parts:

(1) Those relating to the commercial banks

(2) Those relating to the DFIs and

(3) Those relating to the capital market.

The implications of some of the major recommendations relating to the commercial banking system in India are to be analysed below:

Regarding the structure of the commercial banking sector, the Committee has pointed out that the structure of the banking sector needs to be revamped with focus on profitability considerations. The Committee notes, "Despite the commendable progress serious problems have emerged reflected in decline in productivity and efficiency, and erosion of the profitability of the banking sector." The major factors responsible for these are: (a) directed investments; and (b) directed credit programmes. In both these cases, rates of interest that were available to banks were less than the market related rates or what they could have served from alternate deployment of funds. There has been a deterioration in the quality of the loan portfolio which in turn has come in the way of banks' income generation and enhancement of their capital funds. Inadequacy of capital has been accompanied by inadequacy of loan loss provisions... The erosion of profitability of banks has also emanated from the side of expenditure as a result of past and massive expansion of branches, many of which are unremenerative especially in the rural areas, a considerable degree of over-manning especially in the urban and metropolitan centres and inadequate progress in updating work technology. [Report of the Committee-Summary-Para 3]

In regard to the structure of the banking system, the Committee is of the view that the system should involve towards a broad pattern consisting of: (i) 3 to 4 large banks to become global in character, (ii) 8 to 10 national banks with a network of branches to be engaged in universal banking, (iii) the local banks whose operations to be generally confined to specific regions, and (iv) the rural banks (including RRBs) whose operations would be confined to the rural areas. Each public sector bank should set up one or more rural banking subsidiaries, depending upon the size and administrative convenience, to take over all its rural branches, and, where appropriate, swap its rural branches with those of other banks. Branch licensing policy should be abolished and banks be given full freedom to open or close branches (other than the rural ones for the present) or swap their rural branches with those of other banks on the basis of their commercial judgement. "The Committee is of the view that the move towards this revised system should be market driven and based on profitability considerations and brought about through a process of margers and acquisitions." The Committee further notes, "the structure of rural credit will have to combine the local character of the RRBs and the resources, skills and organisational/managerial abilities of the commercial banks." [Report, Para 21, 22].

The claims of the government and public sector on the banking systems resources have been steadily rising through the mechanism of the Statutory Liquidity Ratio (SLR) which today accounts for 38.5 percent of the net demand and time liabilities of the system.

"The Committee is of the view that the SLR instrument should be deployed in conformity with the original intention of regarding it as a prudential requirement and not be viewed as a major instrument for financing the public sector. In line with Government's decision to reduce the fiscal deficit to a level consistent with macro-economic stability, the Committee recommends that the SLR be brought down in a phased manner to 25 percent over a period of about five years starting with some reduction the current year itself. As regards the cash reserve ratio, the RB should have the flexibility to operate this instrument to serve its monetary policy objectives" [Report Paras 4 & 5]. This is bound to improve bank profitability. But the question remains as to whether the Government can afford to do this and what is the appropriate time therefore. A lowering of CPR would mean releasing money into the system immediately. When inflation is around 11%, this would go against the tight money policy of RBI. Nevertheless, it is only in the fitness of things that the RBI should raise the rates of interest on these deposits, which are far below the market rates, in view of the potentiality for improving profitability.

The Committee believes that the Indian banking system, at present, is over-regulated and over-administered. Supervision should be based on evolving prudential norms and regulations which should be adhered to rather than excessive control over administrative and other aspects of bank organisation and functioning. [Para 34]. Most of the commercial bank expansion in volume and in the number of borrowal accounts has been in respect of the agriculture sector. Agricultural credit deployment has increased to a level of over Rs. 14.000 crore and now exceeds the same by the cooperatives. This system of directed credit programmes has contributed to an expansion of agriculture credit in the directions that were considered necessary. However, this achievement has been brought about at the cost of a deterioration of the quality of the lending, the growth of overdues and consequent erosion of profitability. The disturbing growth in overdues is a consequence of the measure of laxity and departure from the principles of sound commercial backing policy and procedure. By far the most serious damage to the rural credit system and one which has contributed to the decline in portfolio quality has been the evidence of political and administrative interference in credit decision-making. "The Committee's approach seeks to consolidate the gains made in the Indian financial sector while improving the quality of the portfolio, providing greater operational flexibility and most importantly greater autonomy in the internal operations of the banks and financial institutions so as to nurture a healthy, competitive and vibrant financial sector. This will, above all, else require depoliticisation of appointment, implying at the same time a self-denial by government and the perception that it has distanced itself from the internal decision-making of the banks and the financial institutions. The proposed deregulation of the financial sector and the measures aimed at improving its health and competitive vitality would, in the Committee's view, be consistent with the steps being taken to open up the Indian economy, enabling the Indian financial sector to forge close links with the global financial markets, and enhance India's ability to take competitive advantage of the increasing international opportunities for Indian trade, industry and finance." [Para 48]

Three major recommendations of the Narasimham Committee which would have an adverse impact on the flow of resources to the rural agricultural sector need to be analysed in this context; reducing the share of priority sector in total credit, phasing out the concessional rate of interest applicable to priority sector lending and segregation of rural branches of the national banks: 'The Committee proposes that the directed credit programmes should be phased out. This process of phasing out would also recognise the need that for some time it would be necessary for a measure of special credit support through direction. The committee therefore, proposes that the priority sector be redefined to comprise the small and marginal farmer', the tiny sector of industry, small business and transport operators, village and cottage industries, rural artisans, and other weaker sections. The credit target for this redefined priority sector should henceforth be fixed at 10 percent of aggregate credit which would be broadly in line with the credit flows to these sectors at present. The Committee also proposes that a review may be undertaken at the end of three years to see if directed credit programmes need to be continued .... The Committee is of the view that the present structure of administered interest rates is highly complex and rigid. The Committee proposes that interest rates be further deregulated so as to reflect emerging market conditions. At the same time the Committee believes that a reasonable degree of macro economic balance through a reduction in the fiscal deficit is necessary for successful deregulation of interest rates.... Meanwhile, the Committee would recommend that concessional interest rates should be phased out." [Paras 7 & 8]

The Committee starts with the premise that directed credit programmes should be phased out and as part of this phasing out process, the share of priority sector in aggregate credit should be brought down from the present level of 40 percent to 10 percent. They have reasoned out as follows. "With respect to diverted credit programme, the Committee is of the view that they have played a useful role in extending the reach of the banking system to cover sectors which were hitherto neglected. The Committee, however, believes that the pursuit of distributive justice should use the instrumentality of the fiscal, rather than the credit system. Therefore, the Committee would like to view directed credit programmes not as a regular feature but rather as a case of extraordinary support to certain sectors in the absence of economic compulsions to make credit available to them and designed to correct perceived imperfections in the credit market. Such intervention should be seen as a temporary rather than a permanent feature." [Report pp. 27-28].

But such abrupt disruption in the flow of agricultural credit to the large and medium farmers would impair agricultural growth. It should be borne in mind that, though necessarily small, in terms of relative contribution to total output, it is this category of farmers which accounts for the bulk of total output. The branches will face difficulties in convincing the borrowers about the righteousness of the matter. Hence, the feasibility of reducing PS credit in a gradual manner will have to be explored. The role of NABARD may require refinancing but in any case not to be minimised. NABARD will have to bring out special refinancing schemes for farmers taken out of priority segment in pursuance of implementation of the Committee's recommendations. The impact of reduction in PS credit on the implementation of the Service Area Approach and the DCP also needs to be studied, as there could be many activities which would no longer form a part of the priority segment as per the recommendations. According to the Directional Paper on the Eighth Plan" "The strategy for agricultural development in the Eighth Plan must aim at not only achieving self-sufficiency in food but also generating surpluses of specific agricultural commodities for export...Agriculture and allied activities on which two-thirds of the workforce are still dependent must continue to receive a major emphasis in our planning effort," Taking the totality of the Narasimham Committee's recommendation, it is amply clear that they reveal an inadequate appreciation of the critical role that the agricultural sector will continue to play in future in Indian economic growth. The ills of the public sector banks cannot be totally attributed to priority sector lending. In fact there is sufficient empirical evidence to show that intervention policies in the financial sector have played a crucial role in some "success stories" of some Asian countries.

On the interest rate reforms, the Committee believes that the medium term objective should be to move towards market determined interest rates. It has, however, advocated a cautious approach to deregulation. In the absence of reasonable macro-economic balance and control of inflation, total deregulation would pose danger. The RBI should aim at simplifying the structure of interest rates. It is often said that the reform in the interest rate structure is the key to the financial sector reforms. Regarding interest rate reforms, the Committee's recommendations are by and large, reiterations of the Chakravarty Committee (1985). A completely deregulated interest rate regime may neither be desirable nor politically acceptable. According to Dr. C. Rangarajan, it is best to proceed in stages so far as deregulation of interest rate regime is concerned. Another question that deserves serious attention is the existence of a labyrinth of interest rates and other inter se anomalies. If interest rates are allowed to conform to the changes in market conditions, this is likely to be more complicated.

Regarding the RRBs, the Committee agreed with the assessment of the RBI Committee (1989). but suggested a different solution, namely, that the sponsor banks should segregate the operations of their rural branches through the formation of one or more subsidiaries which should be treated on par with the RRBs. "The Committee proposes, that while RRBs should be allowed to engage in all types of banking business, their focus should continue to be to lend to the target groups to maintain at a minimum the present level of their lending to those groups." "The Committee would leave the option open to the RRBs and the sponsor banks as to whether. The RRBs should retain their identity so that their focus on lending to the target groups is not diffused or where both RRBs and the sponsor banks wish to do so they could be merged with the sponsor banks and the sponsor banks in such cases should take them over as 100 percent subsidiaries by buying out the shares from other agencies at a token price, and eventually merge them with the rural banking subsidiaries which we have proposed." [Para 22]. Some rationalisation of the structure of rural banking subsidiaries is possible by swapping of branches among banks; the subsidiaries would thus be cost effective. This factor, coupled with the phasing out of concessional lending to priority sectors, the committee hopes, would eventually render the subsidiaries viable.

The experience of IRDP is instructive in this regard. In many cases of IRDP lending, banks have virtually abdicated their responsibilities in undertaking need-based credit assessment and appraisal of potential viability and instead have tended to rely solely on lists of identified borrowers prepared by government authorities. The phenomenon of loan mela was quite contrary to the principles of a professional appraisal of bank credit needs. There was hardly any serious appraisal of credit need, potential productive activity of provision of effective post credit supervision.

The Narasimham Committee on the Financial System has not made any specific recommendations regarding the Cooperative banking or credit system as such, presumably because the entire issue of rural credit had been exhaustibly studied by the ACRC chaired by Prof. Khusro. The general recommendations made by the Narasimham Committee, on such matters as interest rate policy, credit to priority sector and weaker sections of the society, subsidiaries, autonomy of financial institutions, etc., would no doubt, affect the operations of the rural co-operative credit institutions also. In practically all these areas, there is a strong identity of approach between the Khusro Committee and the Narasimham Committee, though the latter has advocated a faster pace of reforms, which would be considered feasible in the then prevailing pre-liberalisation policy environment.

Rural development is as important as industrial development or export growth, but as a subject it is far less attractive a study, than the other two, especially in the current emphoria about the market theology. For instance, not much focus is paid to cooperative credit structure-which seems to fit admirably into the new framework of growth. Although the co-operative spirit has dimmed in recent years it seems worthwhile to explain whether these institutions could be restructured and made to play an important role in rural economic growth. Similarly, if there is a need to forge new institutions especially designed to some rural development, like the proposal for 'Satellite banking' or a separate bank for the tiny sector, these also need to be fully examined. Thus adequate provision of rural finance is so important for future growth that it is not too late to set up a Committee to look into these and related matters.

How many of the recommendations of the Narasimham Committee would be implemented and to what extent, cannot be predicted at this juncture. The Committee has handed a mammoth task, involving a large number of issues, in a record time of less than three months. While some of the basic problems of public sector commercial banking have been ably dealt with and specific action plans have been suggested in the context of new economic set up in India. What is essentially a prescriptic report on the basis of new liberalisation programme, the recommendations are already seen as preemptory.

In a nutshell, the recommendations of the Narasimham Committee envisage far-reaching changes in the financial environment in general and banking environment in particular. These changes signalling a dynamic environment may pose a threat if the banking sector does not change. But if the banking sector also changes appropriately and well in time, the same environmental changes may be turned into opportunities. The prudence of the Committee lies in its recognition that by ensuing competition, integration and autonomy for banks and financial institutions, instead of denationalisation, a level-playing field will emerge. In the long run, this will make the financial system vibrant and efficient. Many of the measures may sound radical, particularly those affecting flexibility of the Government. However, these are unavoidable, particularly if the objective is to sustain the liberalisation measures unleashed in the real sector of the Indian economic system.

The Discussion Paper of the Ministry of Finance, "Economic Reforms: Two years after and the Task Ahead" analyses the financial sector reform of the Narasimham Committee already undertaken and sets the agenda for more to follow over the next three years. A detailed Report by the economists Jagadish Bhagawati and T.N. Srinivasan (JB-JN) on India's liberalisation programme and economic reforms, released by the finance ministry, while enlightening on the reform programme in general is all praise for the insights of the Narasimham Committee and emphasises the need for a speedier implementation of financial sector reform.

At the start of the reforms, the finance Minister stated that the financial sector reforms have to be completed in a phased manner over a period of three to four years. But many unexpected events such as the state abetted securities scam have slackened the pace of reforms as well as underlined the need for proper phasing of the reform measures. Despite the slackening, a critical mass of reforms which could generate a memorandum of its own in the financial sector could be said to have been initiated so far. the sequencing has been broadly on the right lines in that it has not seriously derailed the system through the reform process has undermined the social commitments of banks. Under the reform process, rural credit has been made. "An object of affectionate sentiments shorn of substances' as S. Venkataraman, former Governor of the Reserve Bank of India put it in a recent article, and rural branches originally conceived as focal points of rural development, are being converted into offices for collection of rural savings to be utilised in urban centres. Whether such a pro-urban, pro-rich reforms will be accepted by the rural people constituting the majority remain to be tested.

Agricultural Credit and the Eighth Five-Year Plan |1992-1997|

The importance of rural credit as a vital input for the growth of agriculture and as a prime mover for the development of the agricultural sector in general, is widely recognised. Vital factors such as infrastructure, linkages, developmental initiatives, macropolicies and programmes, Government support and the support services like research and extension alongwith the credit can play a significant role in accelerating the pace of development. The Indian economy witnessed sweeping changes during the Eighth Five-Year Plan and has passed through a fast changing environment in the context of liberalisation, globalisation and structural reforms initiated in 1991. The economy is also adjusting to the changes in the context of acceptance of the revised GATT Agreement followed by the establishment of the World Trade Organisation (WTO). The macro-economic and financial sector reforms have had their own impact on agricultural development, a higher growth rate through accelerating investment in agriculture. Poverty. Alleviation, Employment Generation, maintaining Food Self-sufficiency, Commercialisation of Agriculture and generating surpluses for Export and Import substitution, etc. are the major issues in the Agricultural sector which have to be addressed to by the planners.

In order to meet the economic challenge forcing Indian Agriculture, the Eighth Plan envisaged several strategies, supported by higher plan allocations and greater reliance on private sector investment. However, although credit flow has increased empirically, the increasing demand and the challenging tasks facing the agricultural credit sector would continue to attract attention during the IX Plan period as well.

There is a need for enhancing agriculture production and productivity through higher investment and credit support. A strong, viable and professional system of credit disbursals is a *sine qua-non* for meeting the emerging credit demands adequately and in a timely fashion. Credit support needs to be increased for traditional sectors like minor irrigation, farm mechanisation, rainfed farming, dairy and other animal husbandry activities and also for crop production. All these activities have high potential for employment generation as well. There is a need to bring in an attitudinal change and skill development in the credit institutions to meet the complex demands of the future growth and development, keeping the macro perspectives in view.

The Eighth Plan covers the period from 1st April, 1992 to 31st March 1997. The Plan proposes a growth rate of 5.6% per annum. The Public sector outlay is estimated to be of the order of Rs. 434.100 Crore as compared to the Seventh Plan outlay of Rs. 180,000 Crore. In the light of the above outlines, some of the objectives of the Eighth Plan are as follows:

(a) to make resources available for the priority sectors and their effective utilisation so as to complete projects on schedule avoiding cost and time over runs;

(b). to make clear prioritisation of areas for a smooth operation and implementation of the policy initiatives taken in the areas of fiscal, trade and industrial sector and human development;

(c) to create a social security and through employment generation, education facilities and improved health care provisions;

(d) to create appropriate organisations and delivery systems so as to ensure that the benefits reach the intended beneficiaries.

At the time the Eighth Plan was formulated, the setbacks suffered by the economy in 1990-91 and 1991-92, the programme of structural reforms and the need for fiscal discipline had to be taken into account. It was therefore, observed that, "....in view of the impact of structural adjustment programme, the resource crunch which the public sector is facing, and the need for correcting the fiscal imbalances, it would be prudent to plan more or less for the growth rate achieved during the decade and lay down foundations for higher growth in the future." Thus the growth rate (5,6 percent per annum), and the macro-economic parameters supporting it, were set at relatively conservative levels compared to what may have been possible on the basis of the performance of the economy during the Seventh Plan period, particularly in view of the low base year values attained in 1991-92.

The starting point of the need to reforms on Agricultural Credit is that there is need to bring about an employment explosion in developing countries, if poverty is to be alleviated. To begin with the Indian Case, the Eighth Plan is quite clear in its commitment to near full employment during the next decade. To quote, "the Eighth Plan aims at bring employment into sharper focus in a medium term perspective with the goal of reducing unemployment to a negligible level within the next ten years. Such an approach is now considered necessary also because it is realised that the longer and efficient use of available human resources is the most effective way of poverty alleviation, reduction in the inequalities and sustenance of a reasonably high pace of economic growth" [The Eight Five-Year Plan, Volume, 1, p. 116].

Table 2.2: Macro Indicators

Sl. No. Rate of Growth	*VII Plan*	*VIII Plan*	
		Target	*Likely*
1. GDP at factor cost	6.04	5.6	5.92
(i) Agriculture	3.35	3.1	3.5
(ii) Industry	7.54	7.6	7.24
(iii) Services	7.46	6.1	6.66
2. Prices			
(i) WPI	6.66	-	9.24
(ii) CPIIW	7.96	-	9.34
(iii) CPIAL	7.49	-	9.63

Notes: The date on prices is upto 1995-96.

WPI – Wholesale Price Index.

CPIIW – Consumer Price Index for Industrial Workers.

CPIAL – Consumer Price Index for Agricultural Labours.

Source: Approach Paper to the Ninth Five Year-Plan (1997-2002). GOI.

The actual growth performance of the economy, as shown in Table 2.2, appears to have surpassed the expectations. In the first four years of the Eighth Plan, it has averaged over 5.7 per cent per annum, and there is every likelihood that the Plan may end with an average growth rate of nearly 6 per cent as compared to the target of 5.6 per cent [Approach Paper to the Ninth Five-Year Plan (1997-2002)].

The first four years of the Eighth Plan, therefore have witnessed reasonably good performance as revealed by the macro-economic indicators of the economy in terms of higher than expected growth rate of GDP accompanied by a sustainable current account balance, reasonably comfortable foreign exchange reserves and a moderation in the rate of inflation. Of course the first major area of vulnerability is the prospect for sustained and continuous growth of agriculture. In the agricultural sector the fact that public investment has tended to fall since in the 1980s is well accepted. This was particularly so in the Eighth Plan. "Investments in the agricultural sector, particularly towards creation of irrigation potential has fallen short of targets...the percentage of shortfall in irrigation capacity expansion during the Eighth Plan will be one of the highest during any Five-Year Plan." Empirically the complimentarity between public and private investment in agriculture has been well established. Hence a significant decline in public fixed capital formation in agriculture during this period must be deemed as a major contributing factor underlying the marked slow-down in the rate of growth of private fixed capital formation in agriculture.

In one of his articles entitled, "Credit Support to Priority Sectors—A Macro Perspective" in *Economic and Potential Weekly*, January 24, 1998, p. 147, Mr. N.A. Majumdar notes, "the performance of the economy in the last three years of the Eighth Plan was exceptionally good, with GDP growth averaging nearly 7 percent per annum. This, in turn has bred optimism about future prospects. For instance, the RBI waxed eloquent in August 1997 about growth prospects." "There is a growing recognition that it is possible to achieve and sustain GDP growth of 7 percent or more in the near future. The constraints on growth are no longer the availability of domestic saving or external resources as they used to be earlier.

The limit to overcome growth will be set by physical constraints such as lack of infrastructure facilities and inadequate growth in agriculture." (RBI). "Come October and the RBI had to revise downwards the anticipated real GDP growth for 1997-98 to about 6 percent. This became necessary largely because agricultural growth in 1997-98 is likely to be around only 2 percent, in sharp contrast to growth rate of nearly 4 percent recorded in the last three years of the Eighth Plan...The point is that sustaining a growth of 4 percent in agriculture has become critical to ensuring an average growth of 7 percent or more in GDP. Incidentally, there is a lesson here for those policy makers who seek to attribute credit for the 7 percent growth to the process of liberalisation and to the opening up of the Indian economy."

Table 2.3: Investment and Credit of Agriculture

(Rs. Crores at 80-81 prices)

	84-85	*89-90*	*92-93*	*93-94*	*94-95*
1. Fixed	4287	4191	5259	5550	5886
Capital formation	(8.63)	(7.16)	(8.30)	(8.47)	(8.55)
2. Credit	-	4390	4915	4998	5890
(a) Short-term	-	2684	3270	3415	3964
(b) Medium and Long-term	-	1706	1645	1583	1926

Note: Figures in brackets are percentages to GDP in Agriculture.

Source: Approach Paper to the Ninth Five-Year Plan (1997-2002) – GOI, Planning Commission.

It is true that Indian agriculture continues to remain vulnerable to weather related shocks and determined efforts would have to be made to reduce this vulnerability. This cannot be achieved without accelerating agricultural investment and credit availability which, as shown in Table 2.3, has more or less remained stagnant, growing by only about 2.8 percent per annum, in real terms since the beginning of the 1980s.

Institutional credit has played an important role in increasing the agricultural production. The Co-operatives Commercial Banks and RRBs have been meeting substantially, the production/working capital needs as also those arising from investment credit requirements in the Agricultural Sector with the daunting task of meeting the credit needs on the one hand and maintaining their own financial health on the other. Efforts to strengthen these agencies have been given top priority in the VIII Plan. The Government's commitment to the growth of the Agricultural sector is amply reflected in the acceptance of the huge credit projections of the Working Group (W.G.) set up by the Planning Commission for the VIII Plan. Incidentally, the Agricultural Credit Review Committee (ACRC) had also projected the demand for credit from institutional agencies for agriculture to be of the order of Rs. 57,316 Crore (Rs. 27,866 Crore by way of ST credit and Rs. 29,450 Crore as LT credit) by the year 1994-95.

Policy on agricultural credit has been its progressive institutionalisation for providing credit to farmers for agricultural production and raising agricultural products. As we know that agricultural credit is disbursed through a multi-agency net work

Table 2.4: Flow of Institutional Credit to a Agriculture

Agency	*1992-93*	*1993-94*	*1994-95*	*1995-96*	*1996-97*[+]	*1997-98*[*]
Co-operative Banks:						
Short-term	7170	7839	7250	8331	9750	11500
Medium & Long-term	2208	2278	2156	2148	2729	3275
Sub-Total	9378	10117	9406	10479	12479	14775
Commercial Banks, Regional Rural Banks:						
Short-term	2921	3432	688	6194	7941	9377
Medium & Long-term	2870	2945	8650	5359	8233	10122
Sub-total	5791	6377	9338	11553	16174	19499
Grand Total	15169	16494	18744	22032	28653	34274

[+]Targets * Anticipated.

Source: Economic Survey 1997-98. GOI.

consisting of co-operatives, Commercial Banks and Regional Rural Banks (RRBs). Agricultural loans provided by various agencies rose from Rs. 15,169 Crore in 1992-93 to Rs. 28,653 Crore in 1996-97. The projections for disbursement of agricultural term loan during 1997-98 is Rs. 34274 Crore. Details regarding agricultural credit disbursed by various agencies during the period 1992-93 to 1996-97 and the target for 1997-98 are shown in the Table 2.4.

In order to increase the flow of credit to agriculture, the paid up capital of National Bank for Agriculture and Rural Development (NABARD) was doubled in the fiscal 1997-98. Even after significant increase in overall agricultural credit there is a serious problem of over dues that dampens the flow of credit besides affecting adversely economic viability of lending institutions, especially the Co-operatives and the Regional Rural Banks. However, the recovery of agricultural advances by commercial banks has improved from 54.2 percent in 1992 to 61.9 percent as shown in the following Table 2.5.

Table 2.5: Recovery of Agricultural Advances by Commercial Banks

(Rs. in Crore)

Year (Ended June)	*Demand*	*Recovery*	*Overdues*	*Recovery percent*
1992	9338.31	5056.56	4281.75	54.2
1993	10460.92	5847.33	4613.59	55.9
1994	11231.48	6977.27	4754.21	57.6
1995	11073.48	6629.32	4444.26	59.9
1996*	13009.39	8044.10	4965.28	61.9

*Latest available

Source: Economic Survey 1997-98. GOI.

A review of the flow of institutional agricultural credit during the VII and the VIII Plan periods (upto 1995-96), in terms of quantity as also in relation to the targets prescribed, revealed that during the VII Plan period, the performance of Public Sector

Banks (PSBs) under priority sector lending exceeded the target of 40 percent in each of the years (reaching a high of 46% of net bank credit during 1986-87, with the annual average performance being the order of 44.6 percent). However, since 1986-87 the performance of PSBs started declining significantly and slipped to 37.8 percent (2.2% gap) in 1995-96. The target for agriculture advances under the priority sector (fixed at 18% of net bank credit) was also not achieved and the commercial banks' performance under these advances progressively declined from 17 percent in 1988-89 to 14.3 percent (3.7% gap) in 1995-96. The performance of all commercial banks including co-operatives under ST (Ag) credit slipped from 89.3 percent (VII Plan) to 86.9 percent (VIII Plan) of the WG target for the respective plan periods. The credit flow under MT/LT in nominal terms, is expected to increase from Rs. 18401 crore (VII Plan) to an estimated level of 36644 Crore (VIII Plan) as against the WG target of Rs. 17283 Crore and Rs. 51241 Crore respectively. The declining trend in the performance of banks in respect of investment credit was also found to be more pronounced during the VIII Plan period and the achievement in the disbursement of credit is expected to come down from a level of 106.5 percent (VII Plan period) to a level of 72 percent (VIII Plan target). In terms of the total credit flow, the share of cooperatives increased by 3.3% from 53.1 percent (Rs. 24095 crore) during the VII Plan to 56.4 percent (Rs. 60977 Crore) during the VIII Plan. However, the share of commercial banks to total credit flow declined from 41.5 percent (Rs. 18803 crore) in the VII Plan to 37.8 percent (Rs. 40826 Crore) in the VIII Plan period. On the other hand, the share of RRBs in the total credit flow increased marginally from 5.4 percent to 5.8 percent.

According to the Working Group—Report

(i) The overall position of credit flow in the VII and the VIII Plan periods presents a mixed picture. The picture of credit expansion would have been different with the following attributes:

   (a) The performance of CBs could have been better if the banks had reached the prescribed priority sector target fixed for agricultural lending.

   (b) While the ARDR (Agricultural and Rural Debt Relief) scheme had initially dampened the flow of credit, the banks perhaps could have done better by more effective credit planning for supporting the viable/bankable projects/programmes with the infrastructure/linkage support from the State Government.

(ii) The flow of rural credit during the IX Plan under the priority sector is required to be expended consistent with the projected demand.

(iii) Increased participation of the public sector Commercial Banks may have to be ensured for meeting the short-term Working Capital of Agriculture and also to augment the overall credit flow in addition to the efforts of the Co-operatives and the RRBs. The Co-operatives have already made a welcome beginning in lending to non-traditional activities, including agro-based activities, which need to be given further momentum.

The system of credit dispensation in the country which gradually evolved over the past several decades has now more or less stabilised in the form of a structure (Rural Financial Institutions-RFI) with Co-operatives, Commercial Banks (CBs) and Regional Rural Banks (RRBs). These put together have been meeting the credit needs arising out of most of the land-based operations related to agriculture as also allied activities with a fair degree of success. However, in this effort, they have been beset with several difficulties and constraints which have of late, assumed serious dimensions. We are mentioning here a few of them, such as the radical change in approach to lending for agriculture, emphasis on commercialisation and viability of operations, stress on meeting credit requirements of the 'family' rather than individual need for a 'single window' approach for ensuring speed or credit dispensation, better end-use of credit and its recycling. It would be necessary and essential to strengthen the existing branch net work of banks and improve the efficiency, besides improving the data-base system by induction of adequate technology. For credit related operations, the process of planning and monitoring/supervision of credit under Service Area Monitoring and Information System (SAMIS) needs to be upgraded and made more effective. Strengthening of credit institutions is needed for enchancing credit flow in agriculture to meet the emerging demand.

Considering the limitations of the reach of formal agencies, it is essential to create role-space for informal institutions *i.e.*, VAs, SHGs, NGOs, etc. and other innovative mechanisms for meeting the requirements of agricultural development. Efforts to provide effective linkages between banks and beneficiaries for meeting credit requirements and recycling of rural credit need to be improved. The syndrome of wilful default which ultimately affects the recycling of funds needs to be tackled by tonning up the system including removal of constraints in initiation of legal/coercive action. The implementation of the Comprehensive Crop Insurance Scheme (CCIS) in India has had a perceptible positive impact on the production of increasing the risk bearing capacity of farmers and in recovering from adverse effects of natural calamities. Endorsing the recommendations of the Task Force and the ACRC, the Working Group recommends a feasibility study to be undertaken for setting up a 'Rural Insurance Corporation' to take care of rural insurance covering agriculture and allied activities. The Working Group on Agriculture Credit and Cooperation (Planning Commission) further recommends the constitution of a 'Risk Fund[5] to take care of risks in agricultural financing particularly, for supporting socio-economical development projects/programmes for the upliftment of the weaker sections. It also suggests carrying out a study to evolve appropriate risk coverage mechanism based on international experiences in agricultural financing suitable to the Indian ethos and work culture.

Ninth Five-Year Plan and Agricultural Credit Projection

In the last few years, subsequent to the introduction of economic liberalisation and various structural reforms, the scope and content of credit in the Agricultural sector have undergone a significant change in terms of their demand and need. Encouragement to private/foreign investments in some of the agricultural sub-sectors, increased involvement of DFIs and non-credit institutions in agricultural activities is envisaged to bolster the existing credit support in India. Further, higher credit flow for capital formation

Note: The facts and figures are sourced from Economic Survey, GOI, 1996-97 and 1997-98, publications of CMIE, 1995, 1996; and "Report of Working Group on Agricultural Credit and Co-operation (including cop Insurance). For the Formulation of Ninth Five-Year Plan: Planning Commission" GOI and Approach Paper to the Ninth Five-Year Plan (1997-2002) - GOI. Planning Commission.

and enhancement of production are essential to meet the demands in productivity. In addition, it is also necessary to take into account the problems faced by the grass root level institutions in respect of credit dispensation.

In order to give shape to the tasks to be performed in this direction in the next five years, Working Group on Agriculture Credit and Cooperation (including Crop Insurance) was constituted by the Planning Commission on December 12, 1995 for projecting the credit requirements and suggesting strategic measure for strengthening the co-operative structure during the Ninth Five-Year Plan period. Estimation of realistic credit projections is basically dependent on the availability of a sound data base relating to ground level credit requirements and credit flow, recycling of funds and availability of resources with commercial banks. At long last, public sector banks managed to achieve the credit target only in 1996-97. While credit to priority sectors at 41.7 percent of net bank credit exceeded the target, the sub-target continued to remain unfulfilled. Credit to agriculture was at 16.4 percent, what is more, the reform package has affected adversely the priority sectors in another area, namely, interest rates; With the freeing of bank's lending and deposit rates, the new interest rate structure that has emerged, has become highly regressive and is biased against priority sectors.

In an article on 'Credit Support to Priority Sector – A Macro-perspective' in *Economic and Political Weekly*, January 24, 1998, p. 147—Mr. N.A. Majumdar observes, "The Approach Paper to the Ninth Plan (1997-2002) does accord high priority to agriculture and rural development activities in general, in the strategy for future growth. It is therefore, only appropriate that monetary and credit policies would need to be modified in such a manner that they are in broad alignment with the priorities of the Ninth Plan. Looked at from this angle, credit policy has yet to react to the Ninth Plan priorities. The question that, therefore, needs to be considered is "What are the ingredients that need to be added to the credit policy mix?" NABARD has been playing a major role in strengthening credit support for agricultural/rural development. In order to accelerate the flow of credit to productive sectors in rural areas the RBI raised its General Line of Credit (I & II) from

Rs. 5250 Crore in the current financial year. The share capital of NABARD, which was raised from Rs. 500 crore to Rs. 1000 crore jointly by the Government and the RBI in 1996-97, was raised to Rs. 1500 crore in 1997-99 to enable NABARD to mobilise additional resources from market to rural development. "Priority sectors are and will continue to remain, in the medium-term, the bread and butter, both literally and figuratively, of Indian economic growth. Since priority sectors are critical to high and sustain growth of GDP, it should be the business of public sector banks to support these sectors irrespective of whether there are credit targets or not. Let there be no misunderstanding. When we talk of supporting priority sectors in the Ninth and the Tenth Plans, we are talking of supporting perfectly commercially viable banking propositions; and not of the so-called 'social banking'. Public sector banks' approach to extending credit support to priority sectors in the coming years should be guided by this basic principle." [Ibid, p. 147].

In the same article Majumdar further notes, "The Ninth Plan not only recognises the critical role of priority sectors in the future growth strategy but it also specifically stresses the imperative of enlarging the flow of credit to these sectors. These perceptions are reflected in the following illustrative excerpts from the Approach Paper. Of the nine objectives of the Plan the following two are of direct relevance in this context:

(i) "priority to agriculture and rural development with a view to generating adequate productive employment and eradication of poverty and

(ii) Ensuring food and nutritional security for all, particularly the vulnerable sectors of society" (Approach Paper, p. 16).

On the specific issue of credit to the priority sector, Approach Paper to the Ninth Five-Year Plan (1997-2002) says, "Greater credit flow will be ensured to meet the investment requirements of the farming community for stepping up the growth of production. Efforts will be made to ensure timely and adequate availability of credit, particularly to small and marginal farmers and tribal farmers at reasonable rates so as to enable them to make investments necessary for higher production. Crop insurance scheme as an investment for providing security for marginal and small farmers in rainfed areas will also receive attention during the Ninth Plan. In every district, the RIDF must be used to cover projects which encourage group of small farmers, artisans and landless labourers to organise for skill upgradation, processing, transport infrastructure, quality improvement or centred around large agro-based projects or identified sources of regional, national and export demand," (Approach Paper, pp. 56-57). "Efforts will be made to evolve an environment in which Cooperatives become efficient, viable and competitive. This will be achieved through professionalisation, diversification of activities, including of market opportunities and effective recovery systems. Efforts will be made towards structural changes that may be necessary in the case of non-credit cooperatives to facilitate technology upgradation and acquisition of capabilities, product and design development, quality improvement, marketing, human resources development etc." (p. 58).

Regarding Rural Development, Approach Paper says, "Over the last two decades there has been a considerable decline in the incidence of rural poverty. However, a large nmber of persons continues to live below the poverty line. Hence, there is a need for continued direct state intervention for poverty alleviation, while the programmes for self employment and supplementary wage employment would continue in the Ninth Five-Year Plan, these would be redesigned in order to make them more effective as instruments of poverty alleviation. They would also be integrated with the various sectoral programmes as well as the area development programmes within the umbrella of the Panchayati Raj Institutions.

To make self employment programmes more effective in the Ninth Plan, there will be a shift in strategy under IRDP, from an individual beneficiary approach to a group and/or cluster approach. This would facilitate higher investment levels to ensure viability of project. Further the ingredients of this approach would include development of skills of the poor through an inbuilt training component, upgradation of technology, establishment of forward and backward linkages, availability of appropriate infrastructure and market tie ups. [pp. 58-59]

The main theme here is that priority sectors are and will continue to be the main factor in Indian economic growth. A 4 percent growth in the agriculture sector is a prerequisite for a sustained and continuous growth in the real GDP of 7 percent or more. In the SSI sector capacity under utilisation is as high as 50 percent and one of the main reasons for underutilisation is inadequacy of credit. While the Ninth Plan perceptions clearly emphasise the imperative need for providing adequate agricultural credit support to priority sectors, it is the credit policy which is at fault. Majumdar rightly points out, "The phase 1991-96 could in fact be regarded as the unhappy episode in the history of monetary and credit policies: not only was the quantum of credit flowing to these sectors inadequate but also the interest rate regime became unfriendly. Fortunately the winds of change are blowing in the RBI as the more recent appointment of two Committees to look into the problems of credit flow to these sectors clearly demonstrates. Perhaps this is the beginning of the process of realignment of credit policy with the perceptions of the Ninth Plan" [N.A. Majumdar, *EPW*, Jan. 24-30, 1998, p. 150].

In spite of conscious efforts for the expansion of credit to agriculture, there exists a substantial gap between the demand for and supply of agricultural credit. And the dependence of small and marginal farmers and of less developed regions on informal sources for credit is still quite high. The demand for credit in Indian agriculture must have increased in view of the commercialisation and diversification that has taken place in the agricultural sector for a long time. The credit needs of the rural non-farmer sector which holds promise for the future also have to be taken care of. As per the projection of Agricultural Credit Review Committee (ACRC) the demand for credit both for production and investments would be Rs. 38,999 crore by 2000 AD [RBI 1989]. Estimation of realistic credit projections is basically dependent on the availability of a sound data base relating to ground level credit requirements and credit flow, recycling of funds and availability of resources with banks.

The Planning Commission has set up a Working Group (WG) on Agricultural Credit and Cooperation (including Crop Insurance) with a broad set of terms of reference including review of credit flow to agricultural sector, estimate of the requirements of agricultural sector, measures for development of small and marginal farmers/ scheduled castes/scheduled tribes and other weaker sections and for reduction of imbalances among the regions and sub-sectors facilitating the formulation of proposals for the Ninth Five-Year Plan. While the existing database is not strong enough, some micro-level attempts have been made to collect such data from the grass root level for assessing the credit flow (supply side). The Working Group (WG) endorses the suggestion of Task Force for mounting regular studies for estimation of rural debt and credit requirements with the help of sound database. The projections of demand for credit under five different approaches and supply of credit (agency-wise), as worked out by the Task Force and endorsed and accepted by the Working Group.

Taking cognisance of the future potential and demands of agricultural sector, Working Group on Agricultural Credit and Co-operation (including Crop Insurance) for Ninth Five-Year Plan, 1997-98 to 2002 has estimated that a total of Rs. 2,29,750 crore of credit (both short-term and term loans) may be required by the agricultural sector during the Ninth Plan. In order to assess the quantum of credit supply which would be available to sustain the above estimates of demand, projections have been worked out by the Task Force (Planting Commission) on the basis of growth of deposits of CBs, RRBs and Co-operatives to arrive at the expected level of lendable resources for agriculture after reckoning SLR and CRR requirements, inter-agency deposits (in case of co-operatives), the extent of deposits to be segregated for non-agriculture purposes and so on. According to the working Group (Planning Commission), considering the demand positions arrived at from different assumptions and reckoning the matching supply of resources to sustain these, the following projections of credit to be issued have been proposed during each year of the Ninth Plan period, as recommended by the Task Force and endorsed by the Working Group (Planning Commission) – Table 2.6.

It is evident from the table that about 16 percent annual growth rate in credit flow may have to be maintained during the

Table 2.6: Demand Side of Credit Projections (IXth Plan) – Flow

(Rs. in Crores)

Years	*ST Issues*	*% Growth*	*MT/LT Issues*	*% Growth*	*Total Issues*	*Compound Growth %*
1996-97	*19678*		*9139*		*28817*	
(Terminal Year VIII Plan)						
IX Plan						
1997-98	22500	14.3	10875	19.0	33375	15.8
1998-99	25650	14.0	12995	19.5	38645	15.8
1999-2000	29250	14.0	15530	19.5	44780	15.9
200-01	33500	14.5	18608	19.8	52108	16.4
2001-02	38500	14.9	22342	20.1	60842	16.8
Total	149400	14.4	80350	19.6	229750	16.1
Share of Small and Marginal Farmers in total demand (percent)	55.60		31.70		47.25	

Source: Working Group on Agriculture Credit and Co-operation (including Crop Insurance) for Ninth Five-Year Plan, 1997-98 to 2001-02 Planning Commission.

Ninth Plan period and beyond. This may be a hard task given the growth rates of around 10-11 percent in credit flow achieved during the last decade or so. The annual compound growth rate of 16.1% has been worked out as the minimum projected growth rate to be achieved. The Working Group has also estimated that about 47 percent of the credit demand will be on account of small and marginal farmers. ACRC (RBI 1989) had earlier estimated that small farmers alone account for 50 percent of the demand for short-term credit by 2000 AD. Further there is need to supply LT credit to small farmers to promote capital formation. The attention, as such, needs to be paid to small farmers by the credit institutions in the times to come.

The expected share of the various agencies in the disbursement of credit during the Ninth Plan period has also been assessed by the Working Group keeping in view the average institutional share in credit flow during the Eighth Plan as also considering the health of such agencies and the resources available with them. Accordingly, the following agency-wise shares in credit flow have been considered by the Group as shown in the following Table 2.7.

Table 2.7

	Commercial Banks	*RRBs*	*Total (CBs+RRBs)*	*Co-operatives Structures*		*Total*
				ST	*LT*	
ST	32%	8%	40%	60%		60%
MT/LT	67%	7%	74%	7%	19%	26%

Source: Working Group on Agricultural Credit and Co-operative for Ninth Five-Year Plan (Planning Commission).

Taking into account the shares of CBs/RRBs and Co-operatives have been projected at 40% and 60% for S.T. Credit and 74% and 26% for investment credit respectively, during the Plan period. Strategies may be adopted by the CBs for enhancing the credit flow further to keep pace with overall emerging demand.

Table 2.8

Years	*Total Demand Stock*			*Available Resources for Agricultural Financing*			*Resource GAP*				
IX Plan	*CBs*	*RRBs*	*ST & LT Co-Ops.*	*CBs*	*RRBs*	*ST &LT Co-Ops*	*CBS*	*RRBs*	*Total CBs – RRBs*	*ST & LT Co-Ops*	*Total*
19991-98	47188	6209	28577	47074	4239	21003	-114	-1970	-2084	-7574	-9658
1998-99	55596	7241	33184	56673	5073	24154	1077	-2154	-1077	-9030	-10107
1999-2000	77543	9904	44999	60543	7325	31943	3000	-2579	421	-13056	-12635
2000-02	92001	11643	52685	95197	8790	36735	3196	-2853	343	-15950	-15607

Source: Working Group on Agricultural Credit and Co-operation (including Crop Insurance) for Ninth Five-Year Plan 1997-98 to 2001-02 – Planning Commission.

The Working Group has also estimated demand for credit (stock), the resource (stock) expected to be mobilised by the CBs, RRBs and Co-operatives which are furnished in the following table during the various years of the Ninth Plan period:

Demand and supply side of credit (stock) and the likely resource gap may increase from Rs. 9,658 crore in the 1st year of the Plan to Rs. 15,607 Crore in the terminal year as shown in the Table 2.8. It may be stated that the anticipated resource availability of CBs may sharply decline if they resort to aggressive lending to reach the mandated levels and if they are required to meet the future emerging needs of the sector. Co-operative banks are expected to substantially fall short of the resources required for meeting their share of demand for credit (ranging from Rs. 7574 Crore in 1997-98 to Rs. 15,950 Crore in the year 2001-02). The resource gap of RRBs would be ranging from Rs. 1970 Crore in 1997-98 to Rs. 2,853 Crore in 2001-02. However, resource gap of RBs and RRBs together would be nominal and confined only to the first two years of the Plan period. The likely credit gap in these institutions may be reduced with the refinance support from the NABARD, besides the mobilisation of additional resources from the market by way of deposits and borrowings. The resources to be mobilised by banks from NABARD may be to the extent of Rs. 9,000 Crore – Rs. 12,000 Crore during each year of the Plan period. The CBs on the other hand, will have to enhance their credit flow to keep pace with the overall credit expansion so as to attain the priority sector lending target set for agricultural lending. It is also expected that additional flow of funds to the agricultural sector may be forthcoming by way of private investments, foreign investments and also from non-banking and other financial institutions.

There is substantial increase in the credit flow in the Agricultural Sector. In order to meet the emerging demand, adequate credit dispensation in time assumes greater importance. With a view to meeting the resource gap ranging from Rs. 9658 Crore to Rs. 15,607 Crore in the estimated credit flow of Rs. 229750 Crore during the Plan period, the following measures, as suggested by the Working Group (WG), are required:

(i) Capacity building of ARDBs, PACs and RRBs with legal

mandate and financial assistance for cleansing their balance sheets alongwith organisational development, autonomy and transperancy in operations.

(ii) In view of stronger relevance of and dependence on refinance from NABARD particularly for Co-operatives, strengthening of NABARD with appropriate amendments in the legal framework, increasing financial support (through augmentation of share capital, availability of soft loans and other instruments for resource mobilisation) and organizational re-engineering would be necessary.

(iii) Provisions for Central Plan outlay for NABARD for development of rural infrastructures in public/government sector other than the co-operatives, This would supplement the efforts made through RIDF. (Working Group Report, p. 56).

The Rural Infrastructural Development Fund (RIDF) was created by NABARD in 1995 with a total corpus of Rs. 2,000 crore for giving loans to State government and state-owned Corporations for hastening the completion of ongoing projects. In 1996-97 RIDF-II was set up with a corpus of Rs. 2,500 Crore through contributions from public sector banks which had shown a shortfall in lending to priority sectors. These institutions have been created to give rural credit the status it ought to occupy in the financial system. Welcome as they are, these institutions do not tackle the roots of the two basic problems corporating the rural credit delivery system, namely, high transactions costs and poor repayment performance. It is here that innovative approaches to reorganisation of the system are called for. In the last decade or so, efforts of the well established banking system have been supplemented by dispensation of credit through Self Help Groups (SHGs), an association of several individuals of small means created for pursuing separate or group-oriented activities with credit assistance—besides their personal seasonal savings. NABARD's 'Linkage Programme of Self-Help Groups with banks' has proved to be successful model; though on a modest scale. This arrangement of perveyance of credit to borrowers, hitherto falling beyond the ambit of the banking system on a collective basis through the inter-mediation of efficient/reputed Non-Government Organisation (NGOs) would require to be expanded by monitoring and encouraging NGOs/SHGs. Ensuring availability of credit to the needy and those without access to bank credit through this concept will not only enhance the total credit flow, but is also expected to ease the strain on the overburdened resources of the banking system, improve account servicing, ensure qualitative lending and effective recycling of funds.

There has been an increase in the flow of credit to the agricultural sector from Rs. 11,202 Crore by all agencies in 1991-92 to Rs. 28,653 Crore in 1996-97, and to an estimated Rs. 34,274 Crore in 1997-98. This has been possible on account of more finance extended by NABARD to rural financial institutions, Reserve Bank's increased support by way of General Line of credit to NABARD for short-term credit and the introduction of Special Agricultural Credit Plans by commercial banks for this sector. The Reserve Bank has played a central role in motivating commercial banks to place a special emphasis on agriculture. In spite of these initiatives, there is a perception that investments in agriculture have not kept pace with demand. In the context of the priority accorded to agriculture, and also to give an impetus to the flow of credit, the Reserve Bank of India set up a one-man High Level Committee of Shri R.V. Gupta in December 1997 to suggest measures for improving the delivery systems as well as simplification of procedures for agricultural credit. The Gupta Committee's mandate was to identify the constraints forced by commercial banks in increasing the flow of credit, introducing new products and services, and simplifying procedures and methods of working with a view to enabling rural borrowers to access adequate and timely credit from the commercial banking system. Although rural credit has been an area of policy interventions for nearly five decades, the objectives of policy have remained constant; to institutionalise credit, to enlarge its coverage, to ensure provision of timely and adequate finance to as large a segment of the rural population as possible so as to achieve anticipated growth rates in agricultural production and employment. It is now well accepted that the strategies followed resulted in certain real gains; there was a broadening of the rural infrastructure for great delivery, increase in outreach, reduction in the influence of informal agencies as evidenced by increase in the relative share of institutional sources in the cash debts of rural households and substantially stepped-up credit flows for agriculture and allied activities. On the debit side, quality suffered, overdues increased, repayment ethics were diluted, the recycling of resources decelerated and the profitability and viability of the institutional structure was seriously eroded.

As regards prudential norms and overall inspection of banks, the policy statement has referred to the fact that phased implementation of measures relating to income recognition, asset classification and provisioning has considerably improved the resilience of the banking system. It is proposed to further strengthen the existing capital adequacy, income generation and provisioning norms in the right of the Recommendations of the 'High Level Committee on Banking Sector Reforms' under the chairmanship of Shri M. Narasimham, Government of India, 1998. The second generation of reform could be conveniently looked at the terms of three broad inter-related issues—(i) Actions that need to be taken to strengthen the foundations of the banking system; (ii) Related to this, streamlining procedures, upgrading technology and human resource development; (iii) Structural changes in the system. These would cover aspects of banking policy, institutional, supervisory and legislative dimensions" [Report of the Committee on Banking Sector Reforms, April 1998 Summary Chapter 1].

In regard to the roles of banks and Development Finance Institutions (DFIs), the monetary and credit policy statement has referred to the recommendations made by the Working Group under the Chairmanship of Shri S.H. Khan for Harmonising the Role and Operations of DFIs and Banks [RBI 1998]. To enable Indian Financial Institutions and Commercial Banks to compete in a deregulated and increasingly global market place, a progressive move towards universal banking, supported by an enabling regulatory framework, is necessary. DFIs in India have started moving in the direction of universal baking and increasingly operate on commercial as opposed to developmental considerations. Developmental obligations would require financial support from RBI/Government.

The Committees have presented their reports to the Ministry of Finance and the Reserve Bank of India, respectively. While the Committee on Banking Sector Reforms in its recommendations has reiterated the need to establish ARF, it has also strongly advocated mergers among banks. The Committee further points out that there could be some weak banks that are potentially viable and need corrective measures. In such cases the Committee has suggested the possibility of taking recourse to the narrow banking route as a possible short-term solution to facilitate their rehabilitation. However, if the narrow banking option is not found feasible, the Committee suggests that the issue of closure could well be examined. The Khan Panel Report has also suggested mergers as a short-term solution for addressing the weak bank problems and comes out with a convincing argument in favour of universal banking, as mentioned earlier.

One common element among the Reports is the everyone of them has criticised priority sector lending in the agricultural sector. They have underemphasised the importance of priority sector lending in the Indian economy. One difference is that the R.V. Gupta Committee, which was entrusted with the task of examining the agriculture credit specifically, deals only with one aspect of priority sector lending. But he has not supported the priority sector agricultural lending. Gupta wants to scrap the 18 percent target for agricultural lending and suggests that instead the Reserve Bank should announce absolute annual targets for individual Bank, taking into account the flow of agricultural credit in the previous year. The argument advanced is that under the present system the agricultural sector has not kept pace with the availability of lendable bank resources for agriculture. "As a result the 18 percent limit is not relevant any more", the Committee has concluded. The Narasimham Committee has also turned out to be hostile towards priority sector lending. The earlier Committee headed by him had also pointed out that the priority sector lending to be phased out within three years. But they have forgotten one thing that the basic objective of bank nationalisation was to help agricultural and other small-scale borrowers from the clutches of the private moneylenders, he be a rich agriculturist or a local trader. Whatever reform of the banking system the government finally decides upon, it must make sure that the small borrower, whether an agriculturist or a small industrialist, is not thrown back into the clutches of the exploitative money lender.

It has been argued in this review that the elaborate rural credit structure that has been built in the country over the last fifty years suffers from many serious drawbacks. There exists a vast tapestry of issues, some of which have been discussed here. There is no single magic solution that can resolve them all. Whole-hearted and drastic restructuring of the existing system is however necessary if it is to serve its purpose. It will mean restructuring that requires hard decisions, firmness in the face of political pressures and instilling a sense of responsibility and accountability in each sub-unit of the rural credit institutions and in each individual working in them. Viability has to be the key word in the functioning of the institutions. This is especially so in circumstances where they will have to operate in an increasingly competitive environment. There has to be thrust on mobilisation of local resources—human and capital, for the development of each area. Merely pumping in resources from outside is not going to yield any significant, permanent results. The tendency to depend on the clutches of government support and subsidy has to go. So also top-down dictation of programmes and schemes. Complacency and compulsion have to be replaced by a result-oriented entrepreneur-like attitude.

Our rural economy is faced with serious problems as the current century comes to a close in a couple of years. Most of the problems are carried forward from the earlier part of the century especially since independence. Some are second generation problems resulting from the efforts to solve some of the earlier problems. In India, the rural credit delivery system is in the midst of difficult situation: rural branches of commercial banks are making huge losses, regional rural banks are in the red and the co-operative credit structure has practically collapsed. In a land which can boast of being a pioneer in forging an appropriate credit delivery system, the subject of rural credit has suddenly become difficult to operate. The macro-dimensions of rural credit system have not been appreciated very much and that perhaps explains why global institutions like the IMF and World Bank and even many national policy makers treat rural credit merely as an appendage of commercial banks and not as a central and crucial factor to the financial system. The underlying idea is to integrate the poor people into the mainstream of the development process through the enlargement of employment opportunities; and it is here that the role of rural credit as a catalyst of development comes into full play. Evolution of an adequate rural credit delivery system should therefore form, in developing countries including India, the core of financial sector reforms.

In the case of Commercial Banks, given their vast network of rural branches, the best way to overcome lacunae in the credit delivery mechanism is through linkages with NGOs and financing of SHGs. While one has to be careful about the selection of NGOs and SHGs, a pilot project of such linkage initiated by NABARD has reportedly been showing good results. Linkages of this nature can ensure financial discipline and build a positive relationship between the lender and borrowers. At the same time it should be borne in mind that NGOs and SHGs must retain their informal nature and do not end up as another institutional intermediary. The Gramin Bank of Bangladesh and its credit delivery system are much talked of. Many NGOs in our country have been following similar mechanisms on a smaller scale. More positive efforts in this direction can create a permanent impact at the macro-level. The informal financial sector has deep roots and continues to thrive. Harnessing it for better and greater outreach has to be accepted as a positive and inevitable need.

Dynamism of changing economic scenario in India consequent upon the financial sector reforms and ongoing technological changes in agricultural development would throw open several complex policy options in the 21st century. Hand in hand with restructuring the existing, in the changed context of globalisation and decentralised functioning, the possibility of having small localised banks or single branch Unit Banks needs to be seriously considered and advocated. The advantages and evidences in their favour have been pointed out by the experts on a number of occasions. While branch banking by large banks tends to be characterised by impersonal service and top-down dictation, small banks are expected to have greater flexibility in decision-making, have a local base, utilise local financial resources and provide for local participation in management. The U.S. experience in this regard has been positive. Encouraging the growth of such small banks could be one way of really activating the rural financial market. We are witness to so many private sector banks coming up in urban areas. Why can't rural India similarly becomes a vibrant sector attracting banks and financial institutions?

The problems have been looked at from various angles in this review. Institutional development tends to be highly situation specific and determined by socio-political and economic background. It is, therefore, not possible to present a uniform blueprint for quick action. Local circumstances should have a role in determining the shape of the structure that emerges. What is important is to see to it that there is sufficient freedom for such development. In essence what is being recommended is that the efforts have to be viable decentralised and at the grass root level. Financial self-sustainability is a must for each unit of the system, be it the RRBs, the PACs rural branches of Commercial Banks, informal credit units or Unit Banks. Rural India has to vibrate with thousand of such independent decentralised units. The rural sector has to be seen as a viable market with potential for development. Credit is an entry-point for tapping the resources in an economy. Activating the rural financial market in the right manner offers tremendous scope for long-term development of economy and the country. The deregulation and liberalisation has to be extended further enabling all the financial institutions access resources and credit at rates that ensure viable and efficient operations.

The Tenth Five-Year Plan (2002-07) and Agricultural Credit

Of the various problems ailing agriculture, some that have been most visibly the causes of farmer distress are the lack of

---

Note: The facts and figures are sourced from Economic Survey. GOI. 1997-98; "Report of Working Group on Agricultural Credit and Co-operation (including Co-op. Insurance) For the Formulation of Ninth Five-Year Plan: Planning Commission. GOI" and Approach Paper to the Ninth Five-Year Plan (1997-2002) —Planning Commission. GOI.

institutional credit and a heavy burden of debt on farmers, as well as the absence of a safety net in the event of drought or crop failure. The policy emphasis on agricultural credit on the eve of the Tenth Five-Year Plan has no doubt paid divided as lending to the sector expanded at a faster rate in 2004-05, though a comprehensive crop insurance for farmers remains limited in scope and coverage. At the end of December 2004, institutional credit to agriculture was Rs. 85,686 crore and nearly equal to the credit that flowed to the sector in all of 2003-04, leading the finance minister to remark that the target for the year (Rs. 1,05,000) crore has been surpassed. The target for 2005-06 has been set 30 per cent higher than the previous year.

A recent Report of the Standing Committee on Agriculture points out that, of the 26 major commercial banks in the country, only 8 achieved the target of 18 per cent of net bank credit to agriculture while some achieved a mere 12 per cent. The significance of this becomes clear from the fact that loans from scheduled commercial banks made up 61 per cent out of the total institutional credit to agriculture until December 2004-05. When the Indian economy achieved 5.6% GDP growth in 2001-02, the contribution of agriculture and allied sectors was 5.7% vis-à-vis 2.6% of industrial sector. At the same time, the Tenth Five-Year Plan (2002-07) envisages to realise an ambitious average GDP growth rate of 8% per annum. In order to achieve this, all energies of the country need to be focused on total revitalisation and revamping of agricultural sector and other rural financial institutions to ensure average 7% sustainable growth per annum from this sector alone in next five years.

The Task Force on Rural Credit for the Tenth Five-Year Plan has projected the institutional credit flow to agriculture and allied activities to be Rs. 7,36,570 crore during the period 2002-2007, which is more than three times (320%) the current flow (Rs. 2,29,853 crore) during the Ninth Plan (1997-2002). Similarly, Common Minimum Programme of UPA Government also calls for doubling rural credit in three years.

The public and private sector's shortfall in lending to agriculture is borne by the Rural Infrastructure Development Fund (RIDF), established with NABARD. In 2004, its cumulative corpus of Rs. 28,000 cores was allotted mainly to irrigation and roads both of which ran into considerable time overruns. This year the RIDF, as part of Rs. 50,000 crore Agri-Infrastructure Project, has been marked out to jump start another 'green revolution' in the country.

Let us now look at certain developments in the rural banking sector. During the last 10-15 years, rural credit did not get the attention from the commercial banks and the RRBs which it was getting before the beginning of the financial sector reforms. It will be recalled that the RBI had introduced the target of 18 per cent of the net bank credit for lending to agriculture in 1989 and the banks were required to meet it by March 1990. It is a pity that by March 31, 2003, only 5 out of 27 public sector commercial banks and 2 out of 27 private sector commercial banks had achieved it.

Undoubtedly, institutional credit has been scarce for the agricultural sector rather significantly in the 1990s. This may have been due to corrections introduced by banks for their family lendings of the past to some extent. But a preponderant part of the explanation is to be found in the banks' response to much needed reforms, that is to reduce Non-Performing Assets (NPAs), to improve profitability and to satisfy capital adequacy and other prudential norms. It is unfortunate that the system should allow the banks to regard the task of credit delivery as being incompatible with banking reforms.

Are banks reluctant to offer agricultural loans because their earning potential from these loans has been relatively low? While caps on interest rates charged on small loans may have affected the banks' earning capacity to an extent, the weighted average of interest rates on agricultural loans appears quite remunerative even after taking into account all the elements of cost, cost of funds, operating expenses, and the margin to cover regulatory requirements of provisioning, capital charge and normal profit.

Another very palpable cause for the banks' poor lending to agriculture or to small borrowers is their professional reluctance to operate in rural areas. And this is a very unfortunate issue. Given the option, the scheduled commercial banks will not operate in rural areas. It is a pity since March 1995 after the disbanding of branch licensing policy and the grant of freedom to bank boards, the number of rural branches has declined from 32,981to 32,137 *i.e.,* the closure of roughtly 840 rural branches instead of an addition of at least 8,000 branches under normal circumstances. This approach to rural banking and attitude have created a serious institutional vacuum in rural credit. Surprisingly, no attempt has been made to strengthen cooperatives and the regional rural banks (RRBs) or to build an alternative rural banking structure. These are some of the structural issues, difficult to resolve, but urgently in need of solution. It is no use asking banks to expand rural and agricultural credit base without ensuring that there is an adequate spread of the institutional net work of rural lending.

Table 2.9: An Agency-wise share of credit flow shows in the following table

(Rs. in Crore)

	Credit to Agriculture				
	00-01	01-02	02-03	02-04	04-05*
Co-operative Banks	20801	23604	24296	26959	24471
Regional Rural Banks	4219	4854	5467	7581	9176
Commercial Banks	27807	33587	41047	52441	52038
Total	52827	62045	70810	86981	85686

*April-Dec.

The Economic Survey, GOI (2004-05) has focused, fairly enough, on the plus side to the farm credit and insurance issue but cleverly downplayed some key misuses. It contends that institutional credit to agriculture in 2004-05 is expected to 'substantially exceed' last year's level, if credit flow till December 2004 (of 2004-05) is any indication. Normally, that alone should be enough to uncork the bubby. But not for a farmer-friendly regime. The Survey has optimistically revised the target to Rs. 1,08,500 crore for the year. Some of the optimism on total credit is based on farm loans interest rate reduction to 9% - 8.5% (compared to 14% earlier).

Sponsor banks are now responsible for RRB performance and, in view of the bad Kharif, the financing norms for Rabi have been liberalised.

The National Development Council (NDC) recently adopted the Mid-term Appraisal (MTA) of the Tenth Five-Year Plan. According to them accelerating GDP growth to 8% and achieving a wider spread of benefits is not possible unless we reverse the decelerating trend in agriculture. The mid-term shows that agricultural growth slowed down after 1996. It was 3.2% between 1980 and 1996 and then it slowed down to less than 2% subsequently. The Tenth Plan target was to achieve 4% growth in agriculture and allied sectors against which actual performance thus far is less than half.

It is evident that although the issue of farmer distress lends itself readily to garnering political capital, the seriousness necessary by states to put workable schemes into practice is missing. Though substantial progress has been made in terms of credit expansion, investment in agriculture will be the linchpin growth. However, gross capital formation is still a paltry 1.3% of GDP.

3

Commercial Banks and Agricultural Credit: An Analytical Survey

Developing a strong and sound institutional system for purveying credit to the agricultural sector has long been a major objective of Indian banking policy. Over half-a century ago, the Central Banking Enquiry Committee dealt with this problem extensively. The Reserve Bank of India which was set up in 1935 was required in terms of its statute to pay special attention to agricultural financing to correct a situation where in a predominantly agricultural country the weakest link in the credit chain was in respect of rural credit. In its essential, therefore, the objective was to institutionalise the rural credit structure and expand its coverage as an aspect of freeing the farmer and especially the small farmer from the clutches of the moneylender. Indian policy for many decades concentrated on the development of the Cooperative Credit system as the appropriate agency for agricultural credit. It was fact also that the urban bias and mercantile character of commercial banks made them inappropriate channels for rural credit. This policy frame continued until the early fifties, when the nation embarked on national economic planning. Soon thereafter we had a comprehensive review of the whole question of rural credit by the All-India Rural Credit Survey Committee. That Committee recommended an integrated scheme of institutional rural credit, but with the Co-operative system as its centre-piece. One of the important recommendations of that Committee was to suggest the conversion of the erstwhile Imperial Bank of India into the State Bank of India to be charged with the special responsibility for expanding the coverage of rural credit, but once again, as part of an integrated pattern and by playing essentially a supportive role to the Co-cperative Credit system. This faith in the ability of the Co-operative system to meet the diverse and expanding rural credit needs seems, in retrospect, touching. It was born possibly more out of an emotional attachment to the Co-operative ideas rather than a rational appreciation of the limitations and potential of that movement. Despite the nearly five decades of their existence, co-operatives covered barely 3 percent of the estimated total agricultural credit in the mid-fifties. Since then much progress has been made in the Co-operative movement through purposive State support and direction, and both its membership and coverage have grown significantly, as has its share in total agricultural credit. Yet there appeared little doubt that co-operatives still incapable of meeting the vastly increasing credit demands that were being placed on the system. Furthermore, and not surprisingly in a large and diverse country such as ours co-operative progress was very uneven regionally. There was also reason to believe that despite its laudable objectives, the co-operative agricultural credit system reflecting the rural power structure did not reach out to all classes of farmers especially the small and marginal farmer. There were also many institutional, structural and management weaknesses that surfaced in the operations of co-operative credit institutions, not the least of which was the extent of politicisation of the system. Thus not withstanding the strong support which, following the acceptance of the Rural Credit Survey Report, the State was providing the Co-operative movement, the unfilled gaps in the rural credit system were quire large.

Around this time, that is, in the Fifties and Sixties the country also witnessed a significant expansion in the commercial banking and the strong support an expanding commercial banking system gave to Indian efforts at develping a modern industrial sector. Industrial credit which at the beginning of our planning era accounted for only one-third of total commercial bank credit, claimed as such as over 60 percent of a vastly expanded total, in barely a decade and a half. By the late sixties, however, there was serious concern in India with aspects of distributive justice in relation to growth. The defects of the trickle down theory were being exposed and apprehensions were being raised about widening disparities in income distribution, the growing concentration of economic power especially in the industrial sector and reflecting these, misgivings about the role of the banking system in furthering such concentration. There was a strong feeling that commercial banking policies should be reoriented more in keeping with the principles of social justice without any detriment to the cause of furthering economic growth. Agriculture and small scale industry were two sectors which, it was felt, the banking system had been neglecting, and it was to correct this neglect, among other things, the National Credit Council was appointed in 1967. It provided the framework for the flow of bank credit to the preferred sectors of the economy. Because of the growing demand for credit for agricultural and allied activities and the need to provide such credit through banking channels, commercial banks were for the first time in 1967 called upon, as a matter of national policy, to lend to this sector. As a consequence, the Reserve Bank, in its capacity as the supervisory authority over the banking system in the country, initiated several measures to give a practical shape to the role expected from commercial banks the matter of lending to agriculture.

The subject-matter of this study, is essentially based on the problem of institutionalisation of rural agricultural credit. The emphasis on the regional dimension of the problem is really meant to isolate social and institutional factors that contribute to the slow but steady process of technological transformation of agriculture and the accompanying system of institutional credit that is evolving in the country. Thus the present study has its origin deeply rooted in earlier works on rural credit in general, inasmuch as it was considered useful only after commercial banks themselves as a result of these works took, in recent years, a more serious view of the need to finance agricultural activity. Most districts to-day are the recipients of sizable quanta of credit from commercial banks which go to finance their agricultural sector, even through these form a small percentage of the total credit needs of the sector. The All India Rural Credit Survey 1951-52, the Rural

Credit follow-up Surveys 1956-61, and its evaluation by Dantwala were important contribution to the assessment of the extent of indebtedness of rural cultivating and non-cultivating households, the credit gap in agriculture, and the need for enhancing institutional credit in this sector.

The very first step taken by the Reserve Bank after the policy declaration that public sector banks should increase their involvement in financing of agriculture was the sponsoring of a Seminar on 'Financing of Agriculture' by commercial banks held in December, 1968 in Bombay. The seminar which was attended by the representatives of various groups, covered a wide spectrum of subjects including general aspects of financing agriculture by commercial banks, organisational or other aspects and direct and indirect financing of agriculture. Some of the more important recommendations made by the seminar were:

(i) Commercial banks should play a positive and dynamic role in extending finance to the maximum possible extent to the agricultural sector.

(ii) Banks should adopt a selective area and project approach.

(iii) Efforts might be made so that the privileges and concessions enjoyed by the farmers, such as exemption from stamp duty, etc., when they borrow from co-operative banks are extended when they borrow from commercial banks also.

(iv) It was desirable for Commercial banks to make finance available to cover the entire system of their operations.

(v) Public sector banks should tackle the problem training their staff engaged in agricultural finance.

(vi) A closer dialogue should develop between the Commercial banks on the one hand and the fertilizers manufacturers and distributing agencies on the other, with a view to evolving suitable schemes of credit assistance for distribution of fertilizers.

Several Reports by F.A.O. highlighted the administrative costs on lending to innovative projects in agriculture, so as to allow commercial banks to enter the field, and the social costs of the inflationary effect of such credit creation by commercial banks. A number of government sponsored surveys have gone deep into the problem of rural credit, and the role of commercial banks in meeting the credit needs of the rural sector. The All-India Rural Debt and Investment Survey, 1961-62 estimated asset-group-wise loans per rural household (also for cultivating and non-cultivating household) taken from commercial banks among other credit agencies. The estimates were made for all States separately and for all-India. The findings were in line with what had been revealed a decade earlier by the Rural Credit Survey 1951-52. Indeed, in relation to the total borrowings of the cultivators a small decline from 0.9 percent in1951-52 to 0.6 percent in 1961-62. It was only in Madras and Kerala that the contribution of commercial banks was found relatively more significant, though, even in these states, it was negligible in absolute terms. As a matter of fact, as the Rural Credit Review Committee observes for the whole of the country, even after the commercial banks had overcome their earlier reluctance to carry banking facilities to smaller centres and began to derive deposits from such places which started growing steadily, they had not till recently made any significant progress in fulfilling the complementary responsibility of meeting the credit needs of the semi-urban and rural community.

In the initial stages of their entry into the agricultural sector, Commercial banks were advised by the Reserve Bank that they could deploy an additional Rs. 350 million to Rs. 400 million in financing the sector. As against this target, the increase in the outstanding level of agricultural lending during 1968-69 was of the order of Rs. 1340 million. However, this target-oriented approach created problems of its own. With a view to fulfilling the targets, loans were made without observing the usual and normal safeguards such as pre-sanction scrutiny and arrangements for post-sanction supervision. There were also considerable scattered lending rendering post-sanction supervision difficult, if not impossible. The Working Group appointed by the National Credit Council with a view to evolving appropriate organisational sector for implementing social objectives observed that there were larger institutional and credit gaps in the rural economy and underlined the need not only to mop up rural savings but also for the adoption of a multi-agency approach to meet the growing demands of rural agricultural credit.

It was against this background that the commercial banks were required to come in a big way to meet the production and investment credit needs of agriculture both through direct lending to farmers and also for other agricultural and allied purposes such as distribution of inputs and infra-structure requirements. And the experiment for bringing about inter-structural relationship between the urban –oriented commercial banks on the one hand and the rural based primary agricultural credit societies on the other was introduced as a step in this direction for supply of agricultural credit to fill in the gaps and promoting agricultural development. While even the combined resources of the co-operatives and the commercial banks might be relatively inadequate to meet the demands of modern agriculture, it was obviously desirable that these two major financing institutions should work in co-ordination with a view to avoid unhealthy competition, to ensure financial resources to worthwhile agricultural projects and to see that duplication and wastage of resources were avoided. It is also necessary to ensure that the co-operative institutions would not be weakened by the entry of commercial banks into this field, for the national policy is to promote and energising economic activities in rural areas.

The entry of commercial banks in the agricultural sector coincided with the Nationalisation of banks. In early 1968, the Government of India introduced the Scheme of Social Control over commercial banks. Under this scheme the banks were expected to diversify bank credit more widely and extend credit to priority sectors like agriculture and small scale industry. Prior to it, agriculture occupied a small portion of credit out of the total quantum of credit. The Rural Credit Survey Report put the share of commercial banks at 0.9 percent and by and March 1967, it had risen only to 2.1 percent. Although the banking system had taken certain steps for achieving the objectives of social control, the progress made in this regard was not adequate. With a view to ensuring that the banks were adequately motivated towards a speedy achievement of the social purposes such as meeting the legitimate requirement of the weaker sections of the society 14 major Indian Scheduled

Commercial Banks were nationalised on July 19, 1969. It was expected that the nationalised banks would endeavour to ensure that the needs of productive efforts of diverse kinds, irrespective of size and social status of the borrowers and, in particular those of farmers, small scale industries and self-employed professional groups are met in an increasing measure, and to create fresh opportunities for backward areas in different parts of the country. It was necessary to reorient the concept of security for loans, to pay special attention to the growth potential and developmental needs of local areas and to forge close relations with developmental and term-financing institutions. They were required to intensify their efforts, through a coordinated branch expansion programme, from deposit mobilisation in all parts of the country and from all sections of the people.

Realising the bad effects of the target-oriented approach adopted by the commercial banks, the Reserve Bank, with a view to streamlining the loan policies and procedures of banks, undertook a study in1970 of the methods of operations, policy and procedures adopted by some of the nationalised and other commercial banks involved in agricultural financing. A set of guidelines was thereafter issued to the public sector banks in 1970 enunciating the rationale, policies and procedures for making agricultural loans. These guidelines which pertained mainly to direct agricultural financing by commercial banks, laid down the objectives, effective policies and procedures for making agricultural loans both for crop-raising and for durable capital investment. It has been indicated in the guidelines that banks should adopt an area-based approach and that the agro-economic and agro-climatic situations of the areas, where branches are operating, will have to be kept in mind and the scales of finance to be adopted by them have to be on the basis of local requirements and local needs. While meeting the requirements, the efforts of the banks should always be (a) to improve the quality of lending; (b) to help the borrowers to move on to a higher technological plane; and (c) funnel back into the banking system surpluses accruing to the borrowers or from others residing in the area. Emphasis has also been laid on the banks getting into agriculturally less developed areas, moving away from security-oriented lending to purposive and productive lending and financing small and potentially viable farmers. In the same year, i.e., in 1970, Guidelines were also issued by the Reserve Bank for the indirect financing of agriculture, i.e., financing of farmers through primary agricultural credit societies by commercial banks. These guidelines were based on the policy and procedures followed by co-operative banks in financing such societies.

A significant aspect of the Reserve Bank's Guidelines is the emphasis on the adoption of an area approach by commercial banks for their agricultural financing. This approach aims at intensive and wide coverage of the selected areas around a bank's branch for meeting the total agricultural credit needs of the borrower and for ensuring effective supervision over the use of credit by the ultimate beneficiaries. As a part of the area approach, commercial banks formulated "village adoption schemes" in 1973-74. Under this scheme, which aims at intensive efforts for improvement of the village economy contiguous villages were grouped together and the entire credit requirements of the farmers in these villages for agricultural and allied operations were expected to be provided by the designated branch of a commercial bank. It is ensured that the branch in question is equipped with the necessary technical and other staff who are not only expected to deal with the loan applications expeditiously but also to provide necessary technical guidance and advise to the farmer-borrowers. The scheme thus aimed at the integrated development of the agricultural economy of the adopted villages and at the same time tried to avoid the possibility of overlapping of efforts and resources in the same area by two or more commercial banks, As at the end of December 1978, Commercial Banks had adopted 70,270 villages. The number of direct agricultural advances serviced at the end of the above period was 2.05 million while the loan amount outstanding stood at Rs. 4490.20 million.

One of the main objectives of bank nationalisation was to embark on a branch expansion programme, particularly in the rural areas, with a view to carrying the banking habits to the underdeveloped and unbanked areas. Nationalised banks took energetic steps during the first fourteen years of nationalisation (from June, 1969 to March, 1983) as a result of which the total number of bank offices opened comes to 32,920 (the unbanked centres accounting for 19,898 offices and banked centres for 13,022 offices). By the end of March 1983, the total number of offices of the public sector banks in India was 41,559. Since nationalisation, the population a bank office in India was serving came down from 65,000 to just 16,000. In the process there has also been phenomenal growth of bank deposits. Total deposits in public sector banks at the end of June 1969 were Rs. 3,872 crore but by March, 1983 deposits increased to Rs. 45,914 crore. The most significant change which has emerged during the post-nationalisation era relates to the structural transformation in the sectoral distribution of commercial bank credit. In an effort to effect a structural transformation two-fold national targets were set, first, advances to priority sectors should reach a target of 40 percent of outstanding commercial bank credit by 1985 and second 60 percent of deposits mobilised from rural and semi-urban areas should be utilised in the respective areas.

In 1969, the Reserve Bank initiated the Lead Bank Scheme. Under the scheme, a bank designated as the lead bank in a district was required, among other things, to (i) survey the local resources and potential for banking development in the district and identify centres for opening bank branches; (ii) survey the number of farmers which do have banking accounts or which depend, primarily on moneylenders; (iii) examine the facilities for marketing of agricultural produce, storage and warehousing space and the linking of credit with marketing in the district; (iv) survey facilities for stocking of fertilizers and other agricultural supplies and for the repair and servicing of equipment; and (v) recruit and train staff for offering advice to farmers and for the follow-up and inspection of the use of loans by the ultimate beneficiaries. The lead banks had completed the survey of all their lead districts and the first phase of creation of the financial infrastructure is over. Between July 1969 and June 1979 the total number of commercial bank offices increased by 21, 940 and of these, 16,024 were in rural and semi-urban centres. The next phase was formulation and implementation of development schemes and for this purpose credit plans had been prepared by the lead banks in respect of all the districts. Lead banks had since been advised to terminate these credit plans in December, 1979 and prepare fresh plans covering the period in 1980-82 (which broadly synchronised with the Government's Five-Year Plan) as also annual action plans for 1980 for implementation from January 1980. The district credit plan is a comprehensive block-wise, bank-wise, sector-wise and scheme-wise plan. To facilitate the preparation of these plans, the Reserve Bank had issued detailed Guidelines to the lead banks. Monitoring of the progress in implementation of the credit plans had been entrusted to consultative committees at the district level and Co-ordination Committees at the State level. The overall review of the Lead Bank Scheme is the responsibility of a High Powered Committee at the national level, with a Deputy Governor of the Reserve Bank as its Chairman.

At present, the main idea is to put as much stress as possible on "area-based planning." The commercial banks have been asked to integrate their Lead Bank Schemes with district plans so that credit requirements are met throughout the area. A recent study (1983) conducted by the RBI has revealed that the RBI's directives to Lead Banks following the recommendations of the Baldev Singh Committee had not percolated to the branch level. This prompted the Reserve Bank to issue instructions to the Lead Banks so that the guidelines were strictly followed and a periodical review was undertaken by Head Office of the performance of the branches operating under its supervision. The Committee to Review Arrangements for Institutional Credit for Agricultural and Rural Development CRAFICARD had, inter alia, underscored the need for a review by the Reserve Bank of the working of the Lead Bank Scheme though this Scheme had completed more than a decade of working. The Reserve Bank had, accordingly, constituted a Working Group in November 1981 to undertake a critical review of the working of the Lead Bank Scheme. The Working Group since then has submitted its recommendations which have been accepted by RBI with certain modifications. As a part of follow-up action necessary instructions have been issued to banks and the State Governments in this regard.

Incidentally, it should be pointed out here that in June, 1977 the Reserve Bank of India set up a Committee of Experts (under the Chairmanship of Mr. James S. Raj) to study the functioning of public sector banks. The James Raj Committee's Report was submitted at the end of April, 1978. The Committee's recommendations deal mainly with the problems of branch expansion, lending to priority sectors, efficiency in bank services to the public and vigilance arrangements in the public sector banks. The Committee is of the opinion that there should be a process of selective consolidation of gains achieved in branch expansion by each bank for a period of 3 to 5 years on the basis of the size of the public sector bank as well as its performance in respect of its spread in rural areas. The James Raj Committee made an assessment of the working results of the public sector banks but did not probe deeply into the problems of reorganisation and restructuring of public sector banks.

Banking Commission

The Banking Commission, which was appointed by the Government of India in February 1969 to study all important aspects of the working and credit institutions in India, submitted its Report on February 9, 1972. The Report covers the entire field of institutional and functional coverage of Co-operative Banks, Commercial Banks, non-banking financial intermediaries, indigenous bank etc. In the sphere of co-operative banking, the task entrusted to the Commission was to review the working of Co-operative banks and to make recommendations with a view to ensuring a co-ordinated development of commercial and co-operative banks, having in regard in particular to the extension of the geographical and functional coverage of the commercial banking system. The commercial banking system which has entered only recently into this field has no widespread organisation. The commercial bank system does not possess intimate knowledge of the local conditions and problems and will require sometime before it can build it up to an adequate level. However, the main problems with the co-operative credit institutions in their organisational and financial weakness which means that although the institutions are better spread from the geographical point of view and have better knowledge of local conditions and problems than the commercial banks to supply credit to the agricultural sector, in actual practice, their ability to do so is considerably limited. On the other hand, while the majority of the commercial banks are strong in both these respects not only do they have to go a long way in order to provide the necessary spread in rural areas and to build up the knowledge about problems of financing agriculture in all its diversity but, more important, they have to do all this in addition to meeting the calls on their resources from production units in the various types of industry, trade and services. The problem of co-ordination between the commercial banks and the co-operative banks has to be examined against this background. According to the Report of the Banking Commission, credit gaps are very large in areas where neither co-operatives nor commercial banks have virtually any organisation at the grass-root level. In particular, there is a significant gap in institutional arrangements in respect of small, marginal and sub-marginal farmers and other rural producers which call for a different approach. It is enough to concentrate merely on providing adequate credit, emphasis has also to be given to the supervision of the application of the credit and guidance to the borrower in his operations.

The main thrust of the Commission's recommendations in the co-operative field is the creation of a new type of banking at the field level in the form of "Rural banks". 'Rural banks' would be essentially co-operative in character and would provide services of a much wider range than are now offered by primary agricultural credit co-operatives. Besides performing normal banking business like mobilising local savings and meeting the credit needs of all medium and small cultivators, a rural bank, in the long run, would take up the task of implementing programmes of supervised credit, providing ancillary banking services, supplying inputs and agricultural equipment, providing assistance in marketing and generally assisting in the overall development of villages in its area. To facilitate the creation of a rural banking framework, the Commission has suggested that where primary Co-operative Credit Societies are reasonably well-managed and efficient, they should assume the role of rural banks within the co-operative structure. The facilities of such rural co-operative banks should be made available not only to shareholders but also to new class of members called associate members enjoying the rights of borrowing, though not voting. Essentially, a rural bank would be the primary banking institution to some a compact group of villages covering a population of, 5,000 to 20,000 and in sparsely populated areas, all the villages comprised by a development.

The 'rural bank' could be in the cooperative sector or be a subsidiary of a commercial bank and the Commission has recommended that the Scheme may be tried out on an experimental basis initially. In the cases where viable or potentially viable primary credit societies are not available, the Commission feels it desirable to bring into existence 'rural banks' as distinct entities to be set up as subsidiaries of commercial banks. To enconrage local involvement, where a commercial bank sets up a rural subsidiary bank, the sponsoring bank should invite the residents of the area to take up to 49 per cent of the share capital of the subsidiary. It should, however, be possible for such a subsidiary to revert back to the cooperative fold if considered necessary later on. But the ultimate control will rest with the higher unit e.g., either the commercial bank or the district central co-operative bank or the apex bank as the case may be.

The Commission has recommended that in improving institutional arrangement at the primary level, it is as important to make the structure broad-based as to widen the range of eligible purposes for which credit and other facilities are available. The Commission has also recommended that steps should be taken to reorganise the co-operative structure wherever the central banks are weak. In states where all the district central banks are weak, the structure may be reorganised so as to have only branches of the apex banks. In states where the majority of district co-operative banks are strong, the Commission would not like to disturb the existing structure. District Central Banks, which are relatively strong, should be given a chance to be included among 'scheduled banks'. In the opinion of the Commission, there is no case for setting of a National Co-operative Bank.

A set of recommendations haye also been made by the Commission for effective co-ordination between Co-operative and

Commercial Banks in order to create a widespread and progressive institutional base. The emphasis of the Commission on 'rural banks' is not intended to rule out other methods of extending credit facilities in the country-side through commercial banks. According to the Commission the present commercial banking system of the country is much too heterogenous and the nationalised banks should be reorganised into two or three All-India Banks and five or six Regional Banks. Each of the regional banks should specialise in developing banking services in a broad region. According to the Commission, in the present context, it is necessary to try out various alternatives to assess their suitability of a given area. A sound and progressive system of credit, whether followed by Co-operative or Commercial Banks, should have certain well understood goals. The objectives of restructuring the public sector banks are (a) to have a fair measure of equalisation of both the nature and volume of banking business amongst the different units to be formed on restructuring, (b) to have a compact and geographically continuous area of operation under one bank, and (c) to have for the customers a choice of at least two or three banks particularly in large centres of population. The Commission considers that deposit mobilisation in the rural areas will continue to be the responsibility of co-operative banks in spite of the fact that they have no successful record in this line.

The scheme of 'rural banks' as suggested by the Commission is, by and large, realistic though it lays greater emphasis on cooperation on the grounds that "the Co-operative Credit Institutions have played an important role in many areas of the country, have built an organisation at the grass-root level and have acquired insight into the rural problems. Properly managed and operated, Co-operative banking and credit structure can be a source of strength to the whole credit structure of the economy. Under certain conditions the local participation, democratic management and responsiveness to local needs and urges that co-operative organisations characterise more than the ideal type of institutions to be sought after." (Report of the Banking Commission, Page 173).

Khusro Committee and Commercial Banks

[Extracts from the summary of the Report of the Committee

– The paragraph numbers in bracket refer to the paragraph numbers in the original Report.]

In August 1986, the Reserve Bank of India appointed yet another Agricultural Credit Review Committee (Chairman A.M. Khusro) which submitted its Report in August 1989. (RBI 1989). Until late sixties, the commercial banks with the exception of State Bank of India were largely confined to urban areas. However, with the introduction of social control in 1967 and subsequently, the nationalisation of major commercial banks in July 1969, these banks started playing a substantial role in dispensing rural credit and to this end began opening branches in rural areas. During the period from June 1969 to December 1986, priority sector advances of 28 public sector banks (which account for more than 90 percent of the total business of all scheduled commercial banks) increased from Rs. 441 Crore to Rs. 23,811 Crore and their branches from 6,596 to 36,265. The total number of branches increased over five times and rural branches eleven times. The growth in deposits and loans during this period was about 23 times and 19 times respectively. Thus, after nationalisation, rural people have come to be served quite extensively by commercial banks. (Report of the Khusro Committee, paras 3.01 to 3.06).

The commercial banks are mandated to achieve certain targets and sub-targets under priority sector lendings. Forty percent of the total credit is thus required to be channelled to identified priority sectors such as agriculture, small scale industry, small business, etc. Direct finance to agriculture and allied activities is to reach a level of .17 percent of net bank credit and credit for weaker sections 10 percent. All these targets were achieved by the Banks by March 1988 (Report: Paras 3.07 to 3.09).

One of the objectives of nationalisation of commercial banks was to increase the flow of credit to weaker sections. The Commercial banks' involvement in various poverty alleviation programmes such as IRDP, Differential Rate of Interest Scheme, Self-Employment Scheme for Educated Unemployed Youth and Self-Employment Programme for Urban poor, increased substantially after nationalisation. During the Sixth Plan, the share of commercial banks in IRDP (16.6 million beneficiaries were provided term-credit of Rs. 3.210 crore by all agencies) was about 49 percent of the amount. This share of commercial banks IRDP loans has since gone up to 69 percent, as against 23 percent in the case of RRBs and eight percent in the case of co-operatives. [Paras 3.13 to 3.18].

With the rapid expansion of commercial bank branches in the rural areas, it was thought necessary to emphasise deployment of deposits mobilised by rural branches locally in the rural field. The commercial banks were, therefore, advised to achieve a credit-deposit ratio of at least 60 percent in their rural and semi-urban branches. It was not, however, envisaged that this ratio should be achieved separately for each branch, district or region although banks were asked to avoid any wide disparity between different states and regions, commercial banks as a whole could achieve these targets in respect of their rural branches, although not in respect of some-urban branches. As at the end of December 1986, CD Ratio of public sector commercial banks was 60.5 percent for their rural branches and 51.3 percent for semi-urban branches. An analysis of the regional distribution of commercial bank deposits and advances showed a marked variation in the deployment of credit and mobilisation of deposits. Perhaps this is only to be expected considering the widely prevailing regional differences in resource endowments and infrastructural facilities in the country. Certain measures to reduce regional imbalances have been suggested also by the Committee [Paras 3.27 to 3.33]. The overall recovery of commercial banks in respect of their direct advances to agriculture is at the end of June 1987 was 57.4 percent. Their recovery under IRDP was relatively less at 45.3 percent. There has, however, been variations in the recovery state-wise and bank-wise. Whenever commercial banks geared up their organisational structure adopted schematic lending, improved pre-lending appraisal of schemes and launched recovery drives, the recoveries have improved. [Para 3.38].

Under the Lead Bank Scheme started in 1969, the Lead Bank for co-ordinating the efforts of all credit institutions in the allotted districts for branch expansion and for meeting the credit needs of the rural economy. The various machineries created under Lead

Bank Scheme have, no doubt, created an awareness for better understanding of the problems at the ground level. However, many of these Committees under the LBS have tended to become more ritualistic than functional. To tone up the quality of rural lending by the commercial banks, a new approach known as the 'Service Area Scheme' was initiated by RBI from April 1989. The crucial element of the scheme is the preparation of the branch credit plan taking into account the financial support and infrastructural facilities available in the area. Credit planning for a village or for that matter any area, will be more meaningful only if all the credit agencies in the area, effectively coalesce in the preparation of the credit plan and each agency is given a task to perform in its implementation. It is necessary to have better collaboration between bankers and the development planners in this effort. "We would prefer to modify this 'service area approach' into 'development area approach' especially because it emerges out of the development plan and development-linked credit plan" [Paras 3.39 to 3.51].

As of now, the commercial banks are in a position to absorb the losses of their rural branch operatives through earnings from their more profitable business. Although an increase in the share of weaker section lendings, which carry lower interest rates, puts strain on their overall profitability, commercial banks, as a whole, do make profits. The basic point is that if lendings to rural and weaker sections are to be at concessional rates, there has to be some cross-subsidisation and only a system like commercial banks has, in the Indian context, the capacity for such a cross-subsidisation. The emphasis on the continuance of commercial banks as an important channel for rural credit stems from this consideration [Para 3.59]. Although primary object of bank nationalisation, i.e., increased credit flow to weaker sections and rural areas has been achieved, it has created some strain in the system due to rapid expansion and diversification. Several measures have been initiated to one up and consolidate the commercial banking system. In this context it has been thought to increase the capital base of public sector banks to a level of two percent of their assets by the year 1990, three percent by 1995 and further to around four percent by 2000 as against the current level of 1.77 percent [Para 3.61 to 3.64].

If the public sector banks are to emerge as a strong system to be able to purvey credit effectively and efficiently rural areas in the years to come, they should tackle several issues such as reduced staff motivation, etc. They should be accorded greater autonomy in their functioning. Their rural branches need to be strengthened. They should be allowed to have a higher margin and their equity base should be fortified. The targets for financing weaker sections and the rural poor should be reasonable such as the system can bear. They should also be in a position to protect the interests of depositors with adequate cover to the depositors. The Committee would like to sound a note of concern in this behalf. Unless urgent action is taken on these lines to put the house in order, the magnificent office of commercial banks which has been built over time, would not be able to overt the emerging challenges in financing the rural sector [Paras 3.81 to 3.83].

In the view of the ACRC (Agriculture Credit Review Committee) however, the system has not made such dent in the rural economy, as is evident by the fact that only about 30 percent of the rural families have achieved success or obtained access to the institutional credit system. All in all, in the aggregate as well as for the middle farmers, the credit system has a long way to go, before it can said to be extensively used or begin to change the weak structures of the agricultural economy and of the rural credit institutions. The Committee has pointed out several weaknesses in the system such as recycling of credit, poor deposit mobilisation, defection lending, poor loan recovery etc. The basic weakness common to all the rural credit institutions, however, has been the extremely poor viability. As a cumulative effect of the high transaction costs administered interest rates particularly concessionality in interest rates on rural lending, the net margin on loan was negative (-) 3.21%, in the case of Primary Agricultural Societies (PACs). (-) 1.00% in the case of PLDBz (-) 1.86% in the case rural branches of Commercial banks and (-) 3.70% in the case of Regional Rural Banks.

Service Area Approach

The Lead Bank Scheme was introduced to attain decentralisation in rural credit down to the district level. The area-specifice management of the diverse problems persisting in this field was essential for a vast country like ours. The commercial banks with their widely undertaking branch expansion programme balance the major vehicles for implementation of the scheme. During the initial years, the infrastructure and the branch network of the commercial banks were limited. The district level decentralisation of the rural credit system was, therefore, relevant for that time. But, in course of the implementation of the Lead Bank Scheme, its limitation began to be felt. The credit planners and the implementor being the two distinct authorities, accommodability was lacking in the system. With the increase in the rural economic activities, the credit demand increased and a more clear picture about the actual credit need became necessary.

With a view to removing these deficiencies the 'Service Area Approach' was put up as a more delicate machinery as per recommendations made in the seminar convened by the Reserve Bank of India in 1988. The Field Study undertaken in 1987 indicated that while bank credit had increased in the rural areas both in terms of number of borrowers and quantum, under the existing system of monitoring the end-use of funds, it was not possible to assess whether the increased credit had led to increased agricultural productivity or rural incomes. The study also pointed out that the quality of lending varied from bank to bank and area to area. Where bank branch manages were involved, viable schemes had been worked out, identification of beneficiaries was properly made and other norms of lending were followed, the quality of lending was observed to be satisfactory. However, schematic and intensive area approach was, by and large, on the decline and scattered lending was being increasingly resorted to.

The Seminar, therefore, expressed a view that the time was opportune to move towards a system in which each bank branch could concentrate its attention on specified field to develop productive lending. Such an approach, it was felt, had significant advantages in contributing to timely and planned development of identified areas, monitoring and supervision of credit and its recovery, besides facilitating assessment of impact of credit on agricultural production and income generation. The new approach was also expected to harmonise the banks' efforts in the task of rural development through credit. The Seminar, therefore, recommended identification of 'Command Area Approach' (later called, the Service Area Approach) for giving a new direction to rural financing.

As a result of the vast expansion of rural branch net-work of banks, the average number of villages served by a rural/semi-urban branch has substantially come down and is likely to be in the range of 15-25 villages, against over 300 in 1969. It is now desirable for the Branch Managers to pay individual attention to such a manageable small number of villages. The Service Area Approach, therefore, expects the branch staff to survey the villages in their service area for assessing the potential for lending under different aspects and to prepare annual credit plan, reflecting the needs and potentiality of the area of the basis of the information gained through survey of villages and from local development agencies. The annual credit plans thus prepared will also constitute the performance budget of the branch concerned. The branch plans would be consolidated into block-level plans and later into district credit plans. Planning exercises for rural credit would thus start from the grass-roots level.

The Service Area Approach thus remedies the inadequacies and the limitations of the Lead Bank Scheme under which the Lead Bank Officer (LBO) was preparing the credit plan for the blocks/district as a whole but the branch managers, not being aware of the exact operational area of each branch and loaning potential of each village in their notional operational areas, were not in a position to prepare and coordinate, branch-wise, annual plan of lending. Consequently, there was a mismatch between the preparation and implementation of the credit plan. Under the new Service Area Approach, however, the Lead Bank Officers who have acquired skills in credit planning and preparation of bankable schemes relevant to the district, will have the responsibility of helping the branch managers in preparing their branch credit plans and then consolidating these credit plans into block and district credit plans. Under the new Approach, the Lead Bank Officer will prepare schemes for reasonably large areas such as blocks, will hold seminars for branch managers to explain the details of the scheme and the factors which should be taken into account for determining the number of workable units which can be financed in different villages. The branch manager on his part will study the village data and the programmes of development being undertaken in the villages, and, in consultation with the village level staff, decide the schemes and the viable number of units thereunder, which he will be able to finance in a given time-frame. The annual lending programme drawn up by each branch will then be aggregated into annual credit plan of the block. Under the new scheme of credit planning, the annual action plan so emerging will improve in its coverage and realism and would become a consolidation of realistic plans drawn by implementing branches. The Lead Bank Officer will continue to liaise with the development officers at the district level and pass on to the branch managers, the Government's credit programmes for infrastructure development and linkages in their operational areas on which credit expansion would depend. In the new approach, therefore, the Lead Bank Officer will have a vital and effective role to play as a friend, philosopher and guide to the branch managers, an effective link between the banks and the developmental authorities and the convenor of the district consultative committee.

The Service Area Approach seeks to develop in the rural branch managers the skills to ascertain the economic environment of villages, their resource potential, the needs of the farmers, potential for productive and viable economic activities and formulation of lending programmes, based on the reserve potential, locally available skills, availability of infrastructure and linkages. The NABARD is opening District Development Manager's (DDM) Office in all district headquarters, in the course of the next five years. The district managers of NABARD are also expected to prepare reports on the 'potential linked plans' (PLPs) for the district according to the methodology evolved by the NABARD.

The Potential Linked Plans (PLPs) will essentially guide the Lead Bank Officers in regard to blockwise potential—particularly in the field of agriculture. allied agricultural activities and rural artisans/village industries. In the Block Level Committee (BLC), the Lead Bank Officer and District Development Manager of the

NABARD will have to guide the branch managers in preparing realistic service areas plans. These two officers would emerge as the key functionaries for ensuring the success of the Service Area Approach and are expected to guide the branch managers about the methodology to be adopted for assessing activity-wise credit potential of the service area, on the basis of village-wise data but should not spoonfeed them, as this would defeat the very objective of the new approach. What is sought to be achieved under the Service Area Approach, is to develop the insights of the branch manager into his service area and his capabilities to prepare local budgets in a realistic and data-based manner, so that the quality of loaning would gradually improve. What is aimed at under the Service Area Approach is to develop in the rural banker a sense of independence, capability to scan environment and confidence to draw up his own budget and plan of lending without succumbing to external pressures or looking to others to spoonfeed him.

In the context of the PLPs being prepared by the NABARD, it would be better if the commercial banks loaning in the immediate futures till the problems of commercial banks in the matter or high priority sector ratio and low profitability of rural lending are first looked into, at the highest level. The relations between the DDM and the LBO should also be carefully spelt out, so that the overlapping of their roles would be avoided. To the extent the DDM would spend more time in the District, he would be more helpful than the LBO of RBI, who was, by and large, only a visitor and did not develop much insight into the district economy. The NABARD Officials, through participating in the preparation of the potential-linked plan, would be such more knowledgeable and helpful to the LBO. But their attitude towards both LBO and BMs should not be that of an overbearing superior but of a friend. Such an attitude will have to be carefully cultivated because it does not come naturally to those who work for apex institutions.

The problem of effective coordination was specially taken care of in the design of the Service Area Approach. Need for co-ordination at the lower level was felt in order to maintain overall consistency and avoid duplication of efforts in formulating and implementing the credit plans. With these ends in view, a block level forum called the Block Level Bankers' Committee (BLBC) was set up with all the branches of the banks operating in the block (including DOCB, LDB and the RRBs) and the BDO and his technical officers as the members and the Lead Bank Officer (LBO) as the Chairman. The Senior-most Branch Manager of the Lead Bank (in the block) or, in case of non-existence of lead bank branch in the block, the branch of another bank having maximum presence in the block and designated by the lead bank should act as the convenor. At best one of the Lead District Officers of the RBI and the concerned officer of the NABARD was proposed to attend as many BLBC meeting as possible.

The main function of the BLBC was to conduct quarterly meetings in order to (a) finalise the branch credit plans and aggregate them into block credit plan, (b) review the performance of each branch in implementing the branch and thereby the block credit plan, (c) consider the operational problems, specially with reference to the availability of infrastructure and non-credit inputs, (d) review the progress of implementation of the government sponsored schemes, (e) allocate service area to the newly opened branches in the block and (f) monitor the recovery position. Monitoring received special importance in the Service Area Approach. The BLBC being entrusted with the job, a local system of surveilance was introduced controlling offices for this purpose. This was urgent when necessary consciousness about the new system was not yet developed.

The Reserve Bank of India launched the Service Area Approach from April 1, 1989. These have, however, been some transitional problems which had impeded effective and successful implementation of the approach.

(a) The allocation of villages by the Reserve Bank of India was not always acceptable to all bank branches because some braches felt that some of the villages where they had given sizeable loaning had been transferred to other bank's service area. Sometimes, backward and underdeveloped villages were allotted to bank branches, as against prosperous ones transferred away. What is important is that the bank branches apply themselves with full vigour to tackling the problems of agriculture financing and rural development in the service areas rather than quarreling about the allotment of villages.

(b) The problem of organisational weakness of rural branches of commercial banks has not been pointed out so far. The problem is quite serious, where one man branches had been opened by banks, either in their non-lead areas or in backward districts, where the loaning potential was considered inadequate. The strengthening of branches with field staff and technical staff was also done only in areas, where the banks managements felt there was good potential for loaning. Such neglect of staffing at rural branches highlights the basic problem of rural banking, *i.e.*, unremunerative nature of the rural lending given the administered interest rates and crunch on the profitability of commercial banks in general. Again, the Service Area Approach expects each rural branch to be equally effective in all the villages allotted to them and not to be choosy in respect of rural lending, by confirming it to the high potential areas. Such a rural lending policy of neglecting the backward areas and even in the backward areas, financing only 'high value' loans in selected villages, would not be acceptable under the Service Area Approach because the spirit of the new Approach is more egalitarian and suitable as between one village and another.

(c) Another problem which the banks are facing in effectively implementing the Service Area Approach is that many bank branches which are not well organised to do rural lending, have not yet started financing in their service areas in right earnest. Consequently, the farmers residing in the service areas allotted to such branches, are being served neither by Service Area branches nor by the branches which were earlier financing in these villages, for fear of violating the instructions of RBI in service area. This is likely to create problems in the effective flow of credit in several villages in the country.

(d) The branch managers would also need thorough training and technical support in collecting and interpreting village level data and for estimating the village-wise loaning potential, on the basis of such data. In fact, Service Area Approach will necessitate re-orientation of the role of the Lead Bank Officers and they will have to be trained for this role. The emphasis on training of the branch managers and the Lead Bank Officers also needs to be conveyed to all the banks, so that with the support of the NIBM, they would evolve a suitable training arrangement for rural branches, to strengthen the Service Area Approach.

The Service Area Approach is to be considered as an 'evolutionary phase' in rural lending and a time-bound programme for its success has to be worked out by all banks with full support from the Government of India and the RBI. Service Area Approach is not a magic wand which can solve all problems of rural financing. It is an approach to rationalise rural financing, reduce cost of supervision both by reducing the number of villages in which the bank branches operate and also by avoiding duplication of efforts in lending in the villages by branches of more than one bank. Further, it has to be realised that the approach will become effective only when the commercial banks equip themselves to implement it, which will take some time. So, while it would not be correct to expect all rural branches of commercial banks to switch over to the new approach completely, as on the particular date, it will also not be correct to allow the commercial banks complete freedom not to implement this programme at all, because of their organisational weaknesses. Flexibility should be so construed that the banks will have sufficient time to strengthen their rural branches in a phased programme, details of which can be finalised in consultation with the Reserve Bank of India. But flexibility should not mean abandonment of the Service Area Approach in favour of the present haphazard system of rural lending. Several studies for remaining the effectiveness of the Approach have been conducted. These reveal that the circumstances were not ready to appropriate the maximum benefit out of the scheme. The involvement of staff of both Government offices and the banks was lacking. Professionalism and awareness among the borrowers were inadequate. Under these circumstances, the institutional credit mismatched with the infrastructure and the non-credit inputs reached in the hands of the incompetent borrowers. This has been reflected in the poor recovery and recycling of the bank fund. Notwithstanding its technical soundness and need-based character, the Approach is not likely to success unless the aforesaid shortcomings are removed.

Since the last half of the1980's Indian Commercial Banks slowly began to change their character. Instead of administered system and control, freedom and liberalisation began to be accepted for policy-making and operation. The opening up Commercial Bank with the implementation of the Report of the Chakraborty Committee and the Voghul Committee, the trend got accelerated with the acceptance of the Report of the Narasimham Committee.

Financial Sector Reform and the Narasimham Committee

The structural reforms in the real sector recently initiated and followed with great vigour would be less productive and not so meaningful if not supported by similar reforms in the financial sector. Recognising this, the Finance Minister had rooted the idea of setting up of a high powered committee to go into the details of reforms in the financial sector and its components. Subsequently, Shri M. Narasimham, former governor of the Reserve Bank of India was appointed as the Chairman of the Committee. The Committee submitted its Report in November 1991. The main strand of philosophy which runs through its major recommendations is summed up by the Committee itself in the following sentence: "An efficient and market-oriented financial system could thus be regarded as a complement to market based decision-making in the real sector."

The Report of the Committee on Financial System, 1991 could be said to be directed at Indianisation of the basic changes taking place elsewhere in the world, particularly in those countries which sought help from the IMF and World Bank. Therefore, for a proper appreciation of the changes, we have also to take note of the global trends and changes in the banking industry. However, the winds of change were blowing in India even before the Narasimham Committee. The Ghose Committee Report on new formats for balance sheet and profit and loss statement for banks (1985), the Sukhamoy Committee Report on Monetary System (1985), the Vaghul Committee Report on Money Market (1987), the establishment of Discount and Finance House of India (1988), the series of Two Year Action Plans started in 1985 to improve the operational efficiency and financial viability of public sector commercial banks, etc. are striking features in the process of change. All these changes were largely at the initiative of the RBI which had only limited freedom to introduce effective changes in the financial sector. The crisis of 1990-91 hastened the process of change as it became necessary for the Government of India, which is the major stake holder in banking, to agree to bring about some drastic changes in different areas including the financial sector. For analysing the implications of the Committee's recommendations, these could broadly be categorised into three parts:

(1) those relating to the commercial banks,

(2) those relating to the DFIs, and

(3) those relating to the Capital Market,

The implications of some of the major recommendations relating to the commercial banking system in India are to be analysed below:

1. *Structure of Banking Sector*: It is advocated that the structure of the banking sector needs to be revamped with focus of profitability considerations. Despite the commendable progress serious problems have emerged reflected in a decline in productivity and efficiency, and erosion of the profitability of the banking sector. The major factors responsible for these are; (a) directed investments; and (b) directed credit programmes. In both these cases, rates of interest that were available to banks were less than the market related rates or what they could have received from alternate deployment of funds. This has been a deterioration in the quality of the loan portfolio which in turn has come in the way of banks' income generation and enhancement of their capital funds. Inadequacy of capital has been accompanied by inadequacy of loan loss provisions...the erosion of profitability of banks has also emanated from the side of expenditure as a result of fast and massive expansion of branches, many of which are unremunerative especially in rural areas, a considerable degree of over-manning especially in the urban and metropolitan centres and inadequate progress in updating

work technology. [Report of the Committee on the Financial System – Summary- Para 3]

There should be: (i) 3 to 4 large banks to become global in character, (ii) 8 to 10 national banks with a network of branches to be engaged in universal banking, (iii) the local banks whose operations to be generally confined to specific regions, and (iv) the rural banks (including RRBs) with operations in rural areas. Each public sector bank should set up one or more rural banking subsidiaries, depending upon the size and administrative convenience, to take over all its rural branches and, where appropriate, swap its rural branches with those of other banks. Branch licensing policy should be abolished and banks be given full freedom to open or close branches (other than the rural areas for the present) or swap their rural branches with those of other banks on the basis of their commercial judgement. The Committee is of the view that the move towards this revised system should be market driven and based on profitability considerations and brought about through a process of mergers and acquisitions. The Committee is of the view that the structure of rural credit will have to combine the local character of the RRBs and the resources, skills and organisations/ managerial abilities of the commercial banks. [Report – Paras 21, 22].

Mergers, acquisitions and consideration of banks are likely. However, there may be stiff resistance against mergers from those banks which will be merged. The story of attempts to have harmonious merger of banks, over the years has not been a happy one mainly on account of differences in ethos of these banks. Hence, adequate spadework needs to be done before the entire procedure of merger/ acquisition is given a concrete space. The sponsor banks may begin a stock-taking exercise of RRBs immediately. Now that RRBs staff scales of pay would be equal to those of commercial banks, norms of staff productivity, talent, skill, etc, may be enforced in the case of re-structured rural banking subsidiaries which may undertake variety of activities as the Committee desires. According to certain estimates by the Finance Ministry, 25 to 30 rural banking subsidiaries will have to be floated. Banks may also have to think of a suitable policy to redeploy staff to their rural subsidiaries.

Scrapping of branches, though difficult to undertake, will have to be carried out, if a leaner and thinner organisational set up is contemplated as a facilitator of efficiency and profitability. However, no bank would like to take over loss-making branches of another bank unless the bad/doubtful debts are transferred elsewhere or suitable adjustments are made. In the recent past, the RBI had a proposal to convert loss making branches into branches specialising in housing finance. This proposal may also be looked into.

2. The Committee has recommended that competition and level-playing field should be an essence of financial system. To this end, the Committee has suggested that the Government should remove the disincentives for more dynamic among the private banks to grow. There should be a further liberal policy to allow foreign banks to open branches or subsidiaries in India. Further, Government should permit and actively encourage joint ventures between foreign banks and Indian Banks particularly in regard to merchant and investment banking, leasing and other newer forms of financial services. Foreign banks should be subject to the same requirements as applicable to domestic banks. With equal access to finances and markets, private and foreign banks are likely to increase their operation in a big way, although the fact remains that what character the private banks will take—national, local or even their size will depend upon their capacity for expansion. Corporate giants with enough capital strength may float a number of new banks. Even the NBFIs will be interested in having strategic alliances with PSBs for various financial services/products.

All these would mean increased competition for the PSBs in a big way. The fact of facing competition by the PSBs, so far heavily insulated, has to be accorded serious thought. Otherwise the return on assets of India banks, which at 0.15% is almost the lowest in Asia, will be further compressed by the competitive pressure. This may prove ominous for many of the ailing banks. While the existing PSBs cannot get rid of their existing manpower, the new ones will be starting with a clean denominator. The manpower costs in banking are substantial, as illustrated by some World Bank estimates that they take about 3% of total assets and the cost per million of dollar of assets in India is higher by 50% over Pakistan, 150% over Malayasia, and 300% over Indonesia.

3. With a view to providing adequate functional autonomy to the banks, the Committee has suggested that various guidelines by the Government/RBI on internal administration of the banks should be reviewed to examine their continuing relevance in the context of the need to ensure the independence and autonomy of banks. The appointments of chief executives of the banks and the boards should be depoliticised. Functional autonomy is essential for the banks to operate in a market-friendly environment. Banks, within themselves, should also inculcate a culture of self-dependence, which will help strengthen a sense of primary responsibility. For this, the Committee has highly emphasised the need to place greater faith on internal audit and inspection system of banks. The Committee believes that the Indian baking system, at present, is over-regulated and over-administered. Supervision should be based on cooling prudential norms and regulations which should be adhered to rather than excessive control over administrative and other aspects of bank organisation and functioning. The Committee would also like to place greater emphasis on internal and external inspection of banks...Their main concern should be to ensure that audit and inspection machinery (which will cover the credit appraisal system and its observance) is adequate and conforms to well laid down norms [Report – Para 34].

4. On revamping the SLR, the Committee recommended that SLR requirement of banks should be brought down to 25%, and interest rate paid to banks on SLR investments be increased. This is bound to improve bank profitability. But the question remains as to whether the Government can afford to do this and what is the appropriate time therefore. On the basis of revamping the CRR, the Committee has recommended a progressive reduction in CRR, accompanied by an increase in interest rate paid to banks on CRR in respect of impounded deposits.

5. Analysing the Priority Sector (PS) credit, the Committee has recommended to reduce PS credit to 10% of aggregate credit to the re-defined group as to include small and marginal farmers, the tiny sector of industry, small business and transport operators, village and cottage industries, rural artisans and other weaker sections. The Committee has further proposed that a review may

be undertaken at the end of three years to see if directed credit programmes need to be continued simultaneously, the stipulation of concessional interest to the re-defined priority sector should be reviewed with a view to its eventual elimination in about three years. The 10 percent target is arrived at on the basis of the present share of the re-defined priority sector in aggregate credit. In other words, its relative share is frozen at the present level. So far as large and medium farmers and other categories of borrowers, who would be precluded from the priority sector, are concerned, the Committee recommended that the Reserve Bank and other refinancing agencies like NABARD should institute a preferential refinance scheme under which incremental credit to these sectors would be eligible for preferential refinance.

But such abrupt stoppage in the flow of commercial bank credit to the large and medium farmers would disturb agriculture growth. It should be remembered that, though numerically small, in terms of its relative contribution to total output, it is this category of farmers which accounts for the bulk of total output. There is nothing wrong with directed credit programmes. The ills of the public sector banks cannot be totally attributed to priority sector lending. In fact there is sufficient empirical evidence to show that intervention policies in the financial sector have played a crucial role in some countries of the word. The impact of reduction in PS credit on the implementation of the Service Area Approach and the DCPs also needs to be studied, as there could be many activities which would no longer form a part of the priority sector as per the recommendation. While there is some debate going on in the country whether the percentage of priority sector lending should be brought down, on the basis of the redefined 'priority sector' as recommended by the Narasimham Committee, there seems to be a general consensus emerging that the concessionality in the rates of interest, so long as it lasts, should help only the weaker sections.

6. On the interest rate reforms the Committee believes that the medium term objective should be to move towards market determined interest rates. The Committee believes that 'interest rates will have to be allowed broadly to be determined by market

forces" and hence recommends that the concessional rates of interest of priority sector loans of small sizes should be phased out. It has, however, advocated a cautious approach to deregulation. In the absence of reasonable macro-economic balance and control of inflation, total deregulation would pose danger. The RBI should aim at simplifying the structure of interest rates.

It is often said that the reform in the interest rate structure is the key to the financial sector reforms. Regarding interest rate reforms, the Committee's recommendations are, by and large, reiterates of the Chakravorty Committee (1985). A completely deregulated interest rate regime say neither be desirable nor politically acceptable. According to Dr. C. Rangarajan, it is best to proceed in stages so far as deregulation of interest rate regime is concerned. Another question that deserves serious attention is the existence of labyrinth of interest rates and other interse anomalies. If interest rates are allowed to conform to the changes in market conditions, this is likely to be more complicated.

7. On capital adequacy, the Committee has recommended that the banks and FIs should achieve a minimum 4% capital adequacy ratio in relation to risk-weighted assets by March 1993. The BIs stands of 8% should be achieved by March 1996. An Asset Reconstruction Fund (ARF) needs to be established, which could take over from the banks its position of bad and doubtful debts at a discount, the level of discount being determined by independent auditors on the basis of clearly stipulated guidelines. Based on the valuation, the ARF would issue bonds to the concerned institution carrying an interest rate equal to the government bond rate and repayable over a period of five years. These bonds will qualify for SLR purposes and hence banks' fresh resources will be available for normal lending. The profitable tanks should enter the capital market, while the government should in fact funds to subscribe the capital of other banks. This clearly means that huge fresh capital will have to be injected immediately, which can be done in following ways – (i) by offering shares of nationalised banks to the public, (ii) the subscriptions by mutual funds, and (iii) the Government subscription to the capital. ARF is not a solution to the main problem, but it takes the debt burdens out of the bank balance sheets. The cost will however have to be borne somewhere.

The Committee's approach thus seeks to consolidate the gains made in the Indian financial sector while improving the quality of the portfolio, providing greater operational flexibility and most importantly greater autonomy in the internal operations of the banks and financial institutions so as to nurture a healthy, competition and vibrant financial sector. This will, above all also, require depoliticisation of appointments, implying at the same time a self-denial by Government and the perception that it has distanced itself from the internal decision-making of the banks and the financial institutions. The proposed deregulation of the financial sector and the measures aimed at improving its health and competitive vitality would in the Committee's view, be consistent with the steps being taken to open up the Indian economy, enable the Indian financial sector to forge closer links with the global financial markets, and inhouse India's ability to take competitive advantage of the increasing international opportunities for Indian Trade, industry and finance: [Report-Summary para 48].

How many of the recommendations of the Narasimham Committee would be implemented, and to what extent, cannot be predicted at this stage. The Committee has handled a mamoth task, involving a large number of issues and problems, in a record time of about ¾ months. The prudence of the Committee lies in its recognition that by ensuring competition, integration and autonomy for banks and financial institutions, instead of denationalisation, a level playing field will emerge. In the long run, this will make the financial system vibrant and efficient.

Present Position

The system of credit dispensation in the country which gradually evolved over the past several decades has now more or less stabilized in the form of a structure (Rural Financial Institutions – RFI) with Co-operatives, Commercial Banks (CBs) and Regional Rural Banks (RRBs). These put together have been meeting the credit needs arising out of most of the land based operations related to agriculture as also allied activities with a fair degree of success. However, in the endeavour, they have been beset with several difficulties and constraints, which have of late, assumed serious dimensions. While many of them are covered in the study, it may suffice mentioning a few of them here, such as the radical change in approach to lending for agriculture, emphasis on commercialization and viability of operations, stress on meeting credit requirements of the 'family' rather than individual needs for 'a single window' approach for ensuring speedier credit dispensation, better end-use of credit and its recycling. It would be necessary to strengthen the existing branch network of banks and improve the efficiency, besides improving the data-base system by induction of adequate technology. For credit related operations, the process of manning and monitoring/supervision of credit under Service Area Monitoring and Information System (SAMIS) needs to be upgraded and made more effective. Strengthening of credit institution is needed for enhancing credit flow in agriculture to meet the emerging demand.

The point is that a vibrant credit delivery system specifically designed to meet these development imperatives needs to be evolved. And this issue is as important as the application of the Basle Norms to the commercial banks. After all the financial system should sub-serve these macro development objectives. Public sector banks defaulted on the priority sector target of 40 percent of net bank credit and also on the sub-target of credit to agriculture of 18 percent. The share of priority sectors advances declined from nearly 41 percent in the prereform period to some 37 percent in 1995-96. In fact the share of rural branches in total bank credit declined from more than 15 percent in the second half of the 1980s to some 11 percent in 1996. The credit-deposit ratio of rural branches, which had risen above the targeted level of 60 percent, declined to lower than 48 percent in 1996. These are unmistakable indicators of a sizeable decline in the resources flowing to the rural sector, since commercial banks account for some 40 percent of the total institutional credit to the rural sector.

It is true that the scheduled commercial banks have been playing an increasingly significant role in the financing of development needs of agriculture and kindred activities over the years. A brief analysis of total disbursement of direct loans of Scheduled Commercial Banks classified according to bank group, purpose and region is sought to be provided in the following paragraphs.

Amongst all the Scheduled Commercial Banks, State Bank

of India (SBI) group showed by far the most impressive growth performance in their credit disbursements in 1995-96. The disbursement over the years by SBI group increased spectacularly by 37.3 percent to reach a level of Rs. 3,296 crore. Consequently, their proportionate share in total agricultural credit of all the Scheduled Commercial Banks improved to as high as 35.6 percent in 1995-96; it was 32.4 percent during the previous year. The disbursements of credit by Nationalised Banks as a group rose at a relatively lower rate of 19.5 percent to Rs. 5,529 crore during 1995-96. Consequently, their share in total credit disbursed by all the Scheduled Commercial Banks declined from 62.5 percent in 1994-95 to 59.6 percent in 1995-96. The credit disbursed by Indian Private Sector Banks and Foreign Banks together rose by Rs. 66 crore (17.9 percent) to Rs. 449 crore during 1995-96.

The term loans disbursed by the Scheduled Commercial Banks recorded a significantly higher growth of 30.3 percent during 1995-96, as against 20.5 percent growth in the case of short-term loans. An analysis of term loans reveals that of the total term loans amounting to Rs. 4,646.5 Crore, nearly two-thirds was provided for financing the agricultural activities alone while the remainder one-third was extended for funding allied activities such as dairying, poultry, fishery, etc.

The impressive growth seen in total credit disbursements during 1995-96 was not evenly shared by all the six regions in the country. While the growth of credit disbursements in the Central Regional (61.7 percent), Northern Region (29.1 percent) and Eastern Region (25.3 percent) was higher than the overall growth of 25.2 percent for all the regions taken together, it was relatively lower in Western Region (22.4 percent), Southern Region (16.4 percent) and North-Eastern Region (11.5 percent).

The outstanding advances of Public Sector Banks for the priority sector activities at end-March 1997 stood at Rs. 79.131 crore which marked an impressive growth of rise of 13.7 percent over Rs. 69,609 crore a year ago. The performance of the Indian Banking Sector in 1997-98 showed an improvement in the profitability of 27 public sector banks. There was also a decline in non-performing assets, growth of capital adequacy ratio and diversification into non-traditional banking activities. The domestic financial system was relatively unaffected by the South-East Asian crisis because of its meagre expansion to real estage, short term external debt and a relatively transportment financial infrastructure.

The RBI of India's 1997-98 Report on Trend and Progress of banking in India' highlights the recent review of monetary and credit policy that had provided further impetus and greater freedom to banks in respect of their deposit as well as lending operations.

During the year, both operating and net profits of Scheduled Commercial Banks increased from Rs. 12,239 crore in 1996-97 to Rs. 14,624 crore in the subsequent year. For public sector banks the figure were Rs. 8,887 crore and Rs. 10,269 crore. Net profit of SCBs increased from Rs. 4,504 crore to Rs. 6,499 crore. As a proportion of total assets, net profit rose from 0.67 percent in 1996-97 to 0.82 percent in 1997-98. In case of PSBs, the figures were 0.57 percent and 0.77 percent respectively. Among the PSBs the net profit rates of the SBI group increased from 0.84 percent to 1.08 percent. Interestingly, the net profit ratio of foreign banks declined from 1.19 percent to 0.96 percent for the same period.

The RBI Report pointed out that the quantum of gross NPAs as a percentage of advances of PSBs declined from 17.8 percent in 1996-97 to 16 percent in the following year. Gross NPAs as a proportion to total assets of PSBs declined from 11.8 percent to seven percent. The total assets considered here predominantly consist of loans and advances and SLR investments in addition to other assets. The net NPAs as a percentage of net advances also indicated a downward trend from 9.2 percent to 8.2 percent.

Lack of uniform disclosure practices in various countries has made it difficult to distinguish healthy banks from unhealthy ones, according to the RBI. The differences in accounting standards across countries and the absence of serious penalties for publishing inaccurate information also obstruct a meaningful assessment of banks, the RBI stated in a separate note in the 'Report on Trends and Progress of banking in India, 1997-98. As globalisation of banking increased the risk of contagious effect of banking problems and the need to ensure transparency had become vital for the regulators. PBI said.

In spite of conscious efforts for the expansion of credit to agriculture, there exists a substantial gap between the demand for and supply of agricultural credit. And the dependence of small farmers and of less developed regions on informal sources for credit is still quite high. The demand for credit in Indian agriculture must have increased in view of the commercialisation and diversification that has taken place in the sector over time. Also, the modern concept of agriculture, e.g., agri-business comprising input distribution, processing, marketing, storage, export systems, besides, production sub-systems and the credit needs of agriculture have to be met in a comprehensive manner. The credit needs of the rural non-farm sector which holds promise for the future also have to be taken care of. As per the projection of Agricultural Review Committee (ACRC) the demand for credit both for production and investments would be Rs. 38,999 crore by 2000 AD [RBI 1989]. Taking congnizance of the future potential and demands of agricultural sector, Working Group on Agricultural Credit and Cooperation [including Crop Insurance] for Ninth Five-Year Plan, 1997-98 to 2000-02 has estimated that a total of R. 2,29,750 crore of credit (both short-term and term loans) may be required by the agricultural sector during the Ninth Plan. That is about 16 percent annual growth rate in credit flow may have to be maintained during the Ninth Plan period and beyond. This may be a difficult task given the growth rates of around 10-11 percent in credit flow achieved during the last decade or so. Thus, the resource gap may increase from Rs. 9,650 crore in the first year of the Plan to Rs. 15,607 crore in the terminal year. The Working Group has also estimated that about 47 percent of the credit demand will be on account of small and marginal farmers. ACRC [RBI 1989] had earlier pronounced that small farmers alone account for 50 percent of the demand for short-term credit by 2000 AD. Further, there is need to supply term credit to small farmers to promote capital formation. Due attention, as such, needs to be paid to small farmers by the credit institutions in the times to come.

There has been an increase in the flow of credit to the agricultural sector from Rs. 11,202 crore by all agencies in 1991-92 to Rs. 28,653 crore in 1996-97, and to an estimated Rs. 34,274 crore in 1997-98. This has been possible on account of more refinance extended by NABARD to rural financial institutions. Reserve Bank's increased support by way of General Line of Credit to NABARD for short-term credit and the introduction of Special Agricultural Credit Plans by commercial banks for this sector. The Reserve Bank has played a central role in motivating commercial banks to place a special emphasis on agriculture. In spite of these initiatives, there is a perception that investments in agriculture have not keep pace with demand.

In the context of the priority accorded to agriculture, and also to give an impetus to the flow of credit, the Reserve Bank of India set up one-man High Level Committee of Shri R.V. Gupta in December 1997 to suggest measures for improving the delivery systems as well as simplification of procedures for agricultural credit. The Committee's mandate was to identify the constraints faced by commercial banks in increasing the flow of credit, introducing new products and services, and simplifying procedures and methods of working with a view to enabling rural borrowers to access adequate and timely credit from the commercial banking system. Some of the recommendations are stated in the following paras.

The agreements and other covenants/documents to be completed are complicated and simplification is recommended as has been done by some banks, such as the State Bank of India. All banks may examine their systems, and make modifications within two months, and report compliance to the RBI [Summary of Recommendations – Para 6.05].

The focus of credit appraisal should be an evaluation of the income of the borrower, and a comprehensive assessment of credit needs taking into account track record, credibility, capability, as well as technical viability of the proposal. To ensure quick disposal, at least 90 percent of loan applications should be decided at the branch level. Banks, may, therefore, review the position and suitably modify the powers of sanction delegated to the branch manager. Short-term credit needs of the farmer should include all requirements directly and indirectly related to production, post harvest and household expenses. Repayment capacity should be assessed on the basis of aggregate household income from all sources including crop production and ancillary activities [Report – Paras 6.06-6.12].

In line with the change in approach towards appraisal of loan proposals for lending recommended by the Committee, especially, for investment credit should be simplified and made more relevant for focusing on the income stream of the farmer. The system of disbursing agricultural loans, partly in cash and partly in kind has restricted borrower's choice and given rise to undesirable practices including submission of false bills and receipts. In order to foster an environment of trust, banks may disburse loans for agricultural activities on a cash basis only and discontinue the practice of obtaining bills/ receipts of inputs/assets purchased. The value of security taken should be commensurate with the size of the loan and the tendency to ask for additional collateral by way of guarantors where the land has already been mortgaged should be discouraged. In order to give operational flexibility to the lending banker, margin, security and collateral requirements should not be prescribed by RBI or any other agency and should be left to the discretion of the lending banker. For small loans upto Rs. 10,000 however, the existing guidelines may continue [Paras – 6.13 + 6.14, 6.16 & 6.17 of the Report.]

Self Help Groups have proved effective intermediaries for the transmission of bank loans. Banks should give wide publicity to their preference for financing SHGs, sentisise regional heads and branch managers to the potential for good lending through this route, and training to branch managers in assessing the potential of SHGs and simplification of documents. The efficacy of credit depends on the extent and quality of integration between infrastructural facilities, technological innovations, research and extension support. Linkages should be forged and straightened between extension workers, faculty of agricltural colleges, branch managers and Government departments at the local level through the various district fora [Paras 6.49 to 6.52 - Report].

There is a need for branch managers to have a broad knowledge of agriculture and related activities. At many places, farmers are confused about the type of inputs to be used for crops and can be misled by inputs suppliers. Banks should work out a system by which, information regarding the package of recommended practices for the cultivation of crops specified to their areas is disseminated on a regular basis. There should be greater involvement of panchayats in agricultural extension including provision of training facilities to volunteers and creation of user groups of farmers for acting as modes for technology transfer. Whenever possible rural branches should link up their activities with Farmer's Clubs initiated by NABARD [Paras 6.56, 6.57 – Report].

The rescheduling of a loan instalment during times of natural calamities in regard to term loan should be based on the bank's assessment and should not inhibit the bank from extending short-term production credit to the farmer. Timeliness and adequacy of credit are critical to increasing the credit flow to agriculture. Small loans involve higher transaction and administrative costs. As a result, managers tend to look for larger loans where interest rates are deregulated, while banks seek to equalise the price differential by cross subsidisation. In effect therefore, regulated rates of interest operate as a barrier to the sanction of small loans. As has already been done in the case of co-operatives and RRBs, commercial banks should be free to fix the rates of interest for loans of all amounts [paras 6.59, 7.04 – Report.].

There should be a substantial modification of the Service Area Approach (SAA) so as to provide borrowers a choice of banks as well as bankers a large area of operation. Specifically, borrowers should be free to approach any branch of a commercial bank for credit and it would be for the latter to determine whether or not to do business with the borrower. Banks should be free to operate outside their service area and the responsibility of a particular branch for the credit requirements for a specified village should continue to be made in such a manner that every village is linked to a bank branch for its credit needs. The agenda for discussions at the various fora created under the LBA/SAA viz, BIBC, DCC and SLBC should be radically changed. There should a shift from discussion on service area plans and allocation of targets to providing a forum for greater dialogue between banks and government agencies on matters concerning area development, implementation of new schemes, impact evaluation of technology abortion, identification of fresh schemes for credit dispensation [Paras 7.16 and 7.17 – Report.]

As regards prudential norms and overall inspection of banks, the policy statement has referred to the fact that phased implementation of measures relating to income recognition, asset classification and provisioning has considerably improved the resilience of the banking system. It is proposed to further strengthen the existing capital adequacy, income generation and provisioning norms in the light of the recommendations of the 'High Level Committee on Banking Sector Reforms' under the Chairmanship of Shri M. Narasimham, Government of India, 1998.

Reform of the Indian banking sector is now under way following the recommendations of the Committee on Financial System (CFS) which reported in 1991. Meanwhile, major changes have taken place in the domestic economic and institutional scene, coinciding with the movement towards global integration of financial services. These developments have reinforced the importance of building a strong and efficient financial system. The second generation of reform could be conveniently looked at in terms of three broad interrelated issues: (i) Actions that need to be taken to strengthen the foundations of the banking system; (ii) Related to this streamlining procedures, upgrading technology and human resources development; (iii) structural changes in the system. These would cover aspects of banking policy, institutional, supervisory and legislative dimensions [Report of the Committee on Banking Sector Reforms—April 1998, —Summary Chapter 1].... "The central theme underlying our various recommendations is thus on strengthening of the system within the framework of purposive regulation and a strong and effective legal system. Fundamental to the strengthening the system is the improvement in the quality of the banks' assets portfolios. Banks are repositories of the Community's savings have an economic and even a moral responsibility to deploy these resources in a manner which ensures their soundness even while making their contribution to the furtherance of investment, production and national wealth creation ....Financial sector management and reform is a process rather than an event. It cannot be separated from reform in the real sector. They are mutually reinforcing, sustaining and sustained by each other. Thus an important outcome of financial sector reforms is that it could contribute to greater flexibility in the factor and products markets" [Report –Chapter IX – concluding observations, pp. 75-76.]

In regard to the roles of Banks and Development Finance Institutions (DFIs), the monetary and credit policy statement has referred to the recommendations made by the Working Group under the Chairmanship of S.H. Khan for "Honourising the Role and operations of DFIs and Banks". [RBI 1998]. They have presented their Reports to the Ministry of Finance and the RBI respectively.

While the Committee on Banking Sector Reforms in its recommendations has reiterated the need to establish ARF, it has also strongly advocated Synergetic mergers among banks. The Committee further notes that there could be some weak banks that are potentially viable and need corrective measures. In such cases the Committee has suggested the possibility of taking recourse to the narrow banking route as a possible short term solution to facilitate their rehabilitation. However, if the narrow banking option is found enviable, the Committee suggests that the issue of closure could well be examined. The Committee notes, "Mergers between banks and between banks and DFIs and NBFCs need to be based on synergies and locational and business specific complementarities of the concerned institutions and must obviously make sound commercial sense. Mergers of public sector banks should emanate from the management of the banks with the Government as the common share holder playing a supportive role. Merger should not be seen as a means of bailing out weak banks...Mergers between strong banks/FIs would make for greater economic and commercial sense ... such banks could be nurtured into healthy units by slowing down on expansion, eschewing high cost funds/borrowings etc." [Report –Banking Sector Reforms – Chapter V. para 5.13-5.15].

The Khan Panel Report has also recommended mergers as a solution for addressing the weak bank problems and comes out with a cogent argument in favour of 'universal banking'. An interpretation of the recommendations of the Narasimham Report and the Khan Report as the former advocating narrow banking and the latter forming universal banking in presence of the other, would be an over-simplification of the whole process. Yet, clearly while the CAC Report sees narrow banking as the solution for the weak banks, the Narasimham Report sees narrow banking as one of the possible options to address the weak banks' problems. The Khan Report does not directly address the appropriateness of narrow banking for strengthening weak banks, but favours promotion of universal banking. Both the Narasimham Committee Report (1998) and the Khan Working Group (1998) have in essence cautioned against mergers of weak and strong banks unless they are synergetic.

Still, three Reports Submitted to the authorities in a space of 10 days in April 1998, seem to have arrived at a consensus on the need to phase out priority sector bank lending and have recommended that the banks should part with directed credit programmes. One difference is that the R.V. Gupta Committee, which was entrusted with the job of examining agricultural credit specifically, deals only with one segment of priority sector lending. But Gupta has no sympathy for agricultural lending either. He wants to scrap the 18 percent target for agricultural lending and suggests that instead the Reserve Bank should announce absolute annual targets for each individual bank, taking into account the flow of agricultural credit on the previous year. The argument advanced in that under the present system the agricultural sector has not kept pace with the availability of tenderable bank resources for agriculture. "As a result the 18 percent limit is not relevant any more," the Committee has concluded. The second Narasimham Committee submitted to the Government on April 23, 1998 recommended dilution of the directed credit and stated that "social banking need not conflict with canons of sound banking, but when banks are required by directive to meet specific quantitative targets, there is a danger of erosion of the quality of loan portfolio." The Narasimham Committee (2) has termed out to be particularly hostile to priority sector lending. The earlier Committee headed by him had wanted priority sector lending to be phased out within three years. Simultaneously, the Working Group headed by S.H. Khan, Chairman IDBI, 'on harmonising the role of Development Financial Institutions (DFIs) and banks' recommended an alternate mechanism to be developed for financing these (priority) sectors, which "will aim to balance the need for funds with need to bring better suited structures and specialised skills to bear in dealing with the sectors". This group took the position that "whenever a need arises for commercial funding for certain sectors, the same can be provided by specifically targeted subsidies to that sector". So, this group too was not in favour of directed priority sector lending. But they have forgotten totally that the basic rationale of bank nationalisation was to extricate agricultural and other small-scale borrowers from the tyranny of the private money-lender, be he a rich agriculturist or a local trader.

In pushing for the constitution of an Asset Reconstruction Fund (ARF), the Narasimham Report (2) has again gone on attack against priority sector lending when it observes that there is a higher incidence of NPAs for directed credit. This proposition has not been substantiated with facts and figures, however. Whatever reform of the banking system the government finally decides upon, it must make sure that the small borrower, whether an agriculturist or a small industrialist, is not thrown back into the clutches of the exploitative money lender.

The Indian banking system is yet to become 'internationally competitive, despite various reforms initiated in the banking sector, the Economic Survey for 1997-98 said "Crisis in South-East Asia has underscored the importance of the stronger and more robust financial system, specially the banking system, to handle the new risk of globalisation", it said. Though Indian banks have registered commendable progress in terms of geographical and functional coverage, its performance in terms of operational efficiency and viability skill leaves room for improvement, the survey observed. The survey called for the introduction of Capital Account Convertibility for free flow of capital, but warned that before moving to CAC a sound banking system capable of handling risks should be set-up. With the realisation that poor are bankable and banking with poor is profitable there should be no hesitation on the part of the commercial banks including RRBs to actively pursue micro-financing the poor in the context of adequate spreads that are presently available.

It is true that the banking system in India has taken many steps to cope up with the challenges of the competitive market environment created by the financial sector reforms. After the initial setback, there is an increase in the profitability of banks accompanied by a qualitative improvement in their performance. The adoption of prudential accounting norms has imparted a high degree of transparency in the functioning of the banks. The deregulation of interest rates and rationalisation of the interest rate structure have changed the complexion of banking operations. Banking system is now entering into the second stage of reforms. It is necessary to ensure that banks continue to maintain the required capital adequacy rates, avert the addition to non-performing assets (NPAs) and also expedite the process of technology adoption. While accent would continue to be on profitability, the commitment to social banking cannot be abruptly given up. A judicious blend of the two has to be evolved. Gradually from traditional banking, our banking system has matured into a hybrid banking system capable of delivering the credit needs of heterogenous groups of borrowers. It combines the sophistication of computerised lending into the rustic retailing of rural credit. It has nurtured rich traditions. It has also built up people. It has to carry the tradition further to reach the rest of the population.

4

Co-operative Credit

Promotion of credit co-operatives in the later part of the 19th century was a pioneering effort among many measures taken by the government in institutionalising provision of credit in rural areas. To begin with, it was essentially to solve the problem of indebtedness, usury and a stagnant 'rural economy', with a large peasantry. Efforts to build up the institutional financing system for agriculture commenced with the adoption of the Co-operative Societies Act in 1904.

The Co-operative credit system had by the Nineteen Twenties, become the principal institutional agency for the provision of agricultural credit, both for production and investment. However, as a result of the economic depression of the Thirties the movement suffered a serious setback. But, with the Second World War, which saw a period of economic recovery, the co-operative banking system acquired a place of importance in the Indian Banking System by the late Forties. The Rural Banking Enquiry Committee (1950) made special reference to the role of the Provincial (now State Apex) Co-operative Banks as well as the District Level Central Co-operative Banks. It came to the conclusion that a sound and satisfactory co-operative banking system had come to stay though it had developed them in some states only, but they noted that in other states also the structure was in the process of reorganisation, consolidation and rehabilitation. It was of the view that in regard to functions as well as clientele, there could be a broad division of labour between commercial banks and co-operative banks.

Various Expert Committees have opined that from the point of view of structural appropriateness, there is no alternative to co-operatives at the village level for provision of agricultural credit. The Rural Credit Survey Committee, which was set up by the RBI in 1951, summed up its findings in the celebrated dictum that "co-operation has failed, but co-operation must succeed." It diagnosed certain failures of co-operatives in purveying agricultural credit and made many recommendations, to correct the positions, which among others, included state partnership, effective integration of credit with marketing and processing and management through trained personnel. The Committee also recommended a greater role for the State Bank of India in providing the needed credit support for the commercial transactions of co-operatives. The RBI was required to constitute certain funds to provide financial strength and made the co-operative structure commercially viable. The Committee showed that, in 1951-52, the private credit agencies taken together (excluding commercial banks) supplied 93 percent of the total amount borrowed by cultivators, that, of the total borrowing by cultivators, roughly 50 percent was for family expenditure, 28 percent for capital expenditure on farm, and 10 percent for current farm expenditure. Regarding the long-term credit, the Planning Commission had pointed out that "a major part of the advances made hitherto by the Land Mortgage Banks were for repayment of old debts" [Planning Commission 1953. pp. 234-49].

In the structure of co-operatives agricultural credit prescribed by the Committee, there was to be a state co-operative bank, a central land mortgage bank, and a state co-operative marketing society at the apex in each state. At the district level, there was to be preferably a district central co-operative bank or a branch of a State Co-operative Bank, a primary land mortgage bank, and a district marketing society. At the village level there were to be large-sized primary agricultural credit societies, primary land mortgage banks, grain banks, and primary marketing societies. The proposed State Bank of India would help in financing of individual co-operative marketing and processing societies. The Planning Commission accepted the recommendations and under the Second

Five-Year Plan (1956-61) Co-operative Development Schemes were drawn up in all States and the Agricultural Credit Department of the Reserve Bank of India came forward as a friend, philosopher and guide of the co-operative movement in our country. The Survey revealed that co-operative credit, in spite of their existence for over 50 years, accounted for only 3.1 percent of the total borrowings of the cultivators. The Survey further observed that agricultural credit, as supplied by different agencies, fell short of the right amount, was not of right type and by the criterian of need often failed to reach the right people. The Survey took great pains in tracing the failure of the co-operative movement in India to fundamental underlying causes. It concluded that the movement never had any chance of strengthening itself in the unfavourable economic-cum-social climate obtaining in the country as the "heritage of a colonial economy" which shifted the focus of organised private financial power to urban areas with a wholly urban-bias in its outlook".

Rural Credit Review Committees

Just before the commencement of the Fourth Five-Year Plan (1969-74) came the All-India Rural Credit Review which is an important landmark in the history of the Co-operative Movement in India. All-India Rural Credit Review Committee set up by the RBI in 1968, made a very comprehensive review of the Co-operative movement in India and made some important suggestions for improving co-operatives in India. The Committee reported that for various reasons the performance of the co-operatives had not measured up to the expectations and it came to the conclusion that there was need for some supplementary effort, so that agricultural production did not suffer. It, therefore, recommended a multi-agency approach to rural credit. With the establishment of the regional rural banks commencing from 1975, one more constitutional device was adopted to the banking structure.

The reorganisation of rural credit in the Reserve Bank, involving the establishment of an Agricultural Credit Board; the setting up of a Small Farmers' Development Agency in selected districts throughout the Country; the creation of a Rural Electrification Corporation which, among other things, is to benefit undeveloped areas with an agricultural potential; the formulation of a more active and much bigger role for the Agricultural Refinance Corporation along with the enlargement of its resources, and the adoption of various measures for ensuring the timely and adequate flow of credit for agriculture through cooperative and commercial banks –these are among the highlights of the recommendations made by the All-India Rural.Credit Review Committee. Some of these proposals –notably those concerning the Small Farmers' Development Agency, the Rural Electrification Corporation and the Agricultural Refinance Corporation were included both in the Fourth Five-Year Plan and in the Central Budget for 1969-70 and are in the process of implementation.

While demand for credit was going up, supply was markedly lagging behind. Recalling the Integrated Scheme of Rural Credit put forward by the Rural Credit Survey Committee, the Review Committee referred to the earlier assumption that co-operatives, with State participation in share capital and various related measures, would be able to take other in due course the responsibility of providing loans to all credit-worthy farmers. The Committee emphasised that, while reorganisation of co-operative credit should be pursued and the Integrated Scheme implemented vigorously – in stead of half-heartedly as in some aspects hitherto – the progress of agriculture could not be to the progress of co-operative credit and that, therefore, efforts should not be concentrated solely in the co-operative sector. The Committee pointed out that the co-operatives would be all the better, and the farmer would be better served, if other institutions co-exist with the co-operative organisation in healthy competition.

They year 1969 brought about a radical change in the policy and operations of agricultural credit mainly in two directions, one, multi-agency approach to agricultural credit and two, more finance to weaker sections of the community. These were as a result of reported findings of the Review Committee which had observed that the progress of implementation of the integrated scheme of rural credit was bright only in certain parts of the country; that there were regional disparities and imbalances in the development of rural agricultural credit; that the weaker sections of the community did not get the benefit of the co-operative finance to a desired extent; that there were large and widening credit gaps; and that, co-operatives were unable to cope with the demand. The Review Committee recommended, in essence, a multi-agency approach to agricultural financing by inducting commercial banks, which had already been nationalised to meet the growing need in the agricultural sector. This is all the more true after the nationalisation of six more private sector banks in 1980. The aspirations of the people behind bringing the banks mostly under state ownership were *inter alia*, to make them instrumental in the development of the rural sector and to meet the credit needs of genuine production activities in the small-scale industrial sector and agriculture. The problems of poverty and unemployment in the rural sector were sought to be attacked through various schemes in which banking was accorded a vital role. Each district was allotted to one commercial bank called the 'lead' bank which survey the resources and potential for banking development in that district, offer advice to small borrowers, particulars cultivators, assist other primary lending agencies, and maintain liaison with government and quasi-government agencies.

Besides undertaking financing of individual agriculturists directly, the commercial banks were also involved in financing the farming community through the primary agricultural credit societies. A scheme for such financing was introduced by the Reserve Bank of India in June 1970. The objective of the scheme was to meet the wide gaps between the demand for short and medium-term agricultural credit and the credit actually provided by the co-operative credit agencies. The banks would advance short and medium-term credit only through the primary credit societies while they could provide long-term credit directly. In November 1972, the Committee of the All-India Debt and Investment Survey (1971-72), RBI, in its analysis found that, although the commercial banks did provide the necessary agricultural finance, they did not pay much attention to the revitalisation of the societies and professionalisation of the management.

As regards the causes of overdue, the Study Team on Overdues (1974) has classified them as (1) external, *i.e.*, those which are beyond the control of the lending institutions, like the occurrence of natural calamity, irrigation facilities and cropping pattern and (2) internal, i.e., those relating to organisational and supervisory arrangements obtaining within the institution. The Study Team's analysis shows that there has been lack of direct and positive relationship between external factors and the level and trends of overdues. The Study Team has observed, "Experience has, by and large belied the assumption that local leaders of the co-operative movement would work with a great sense of responsibility and zeal to ensure the recovery of the loans of their own institutions," Defective lending policies of the co-operatives, especially inadequate and untimely creditor over-financing or lack of supervision over the end-use of credit, fixation of unrealistic due dates and financing of defaulters combined with apathy of the managements in taking quick actions against recalcitrant members, and lack of support from State Governments had encouraged defaults and lend to the piling up of overdues [RBI 1974, pp. 224-25].

The Sixth Five-Year Plan (1980-85) pointed out that mounting overdues had clogged the structure of co-operative credit. At the end of June 1985 the percentage of overdues to demand at the PACs level was around 40 percent while at the level of LDBs it was around 42 percent. It was worse in the case of RRBs and Commercial banks at around 50 percent. The health of the agricultural credit institutions, both cooperatives and commercial banks, was in a very bad state in many parts of the country. Willful default and overdues were mounting even in cooperatively progressive states like Gujarat and Maharashtra.

Committee after Committee had pointed out these defects but they ended up recommending bypasses to let the credit flow round the overdues acting on the dictum 'credit should be given not only where it is due but also where it is overdue'. But, now a new development had entered the system. By writing off agriculture loans and providing subsidies out of the state exchequer, some states had set a bad example. According to the Seventh Plan, if this trend was not reversed and if banks were reduced to institutions providing grants rather than recycling credit, the banking system would not be able to meet the credit needs of agriculture in future [Planning Commission 1985, Vol. II, p. 17].

The Sixth Five-Year Plan (1980-85) endorsed the setting up of the NABARD and NABARD was established by an act of Parliament in July 1982 "for providing credit for the promotion of agriculture, small scale industries, cottage and village industries, handicrafts and other rural crafts and other allied economic activities in rural areas with a view to promoting integrated rural development and securing prosperity of rural areas".

Khusro Committee and Restructuring of the Co-operatives

In August 1986, the Reserve Bank of India appointed yet another Agricultural Credit Review Committee (Chairman A.M. Khusro) which submitted its Report in August 1989 [RBI 1989]. The Report is the result of in-depth study and fieldwork done by a top level Expert Committee appointed by the Government of India/Reserve Bank/World Bank under the chairmanship of A.M. Khusro.

The co-operative sector has to be strengthened on the basis of the specific recommendations of the Khusro Committee. In spite of the entry of commercial banks into rural credit, with superior resources in money and men, these grass-root level co-operative organisations have held their own and continue to occupy an important place in the rural credit structure, though their performance in the matter of deposit mobilisation or recovery of dues is not satisfactory. The streamlining of commercial banks is relatively easy as they are bureaucratic institutions whereas the co-operatives are democratic institutions and, as such, face many hurdles in restructuring that set-up. Further, while non-credit cooperatives are left on their own, the rural credit structure has more or less become another government wing. It should also be noted that while we have shown our expertise in running efficiently higher level institutions, we have not been successful in developing the grass-roots level rural credit set-up both in the co-operative and commercial banking sector.

As a result of various efforts made following the Rural Credit Survey Committee Report in 1954, there has been improvement in the structure of rural co-operative system but the overall quality of co-operative character and operational standard deteriorated owing to "the politicalisation, officialisation, mass supersessions, low margins and lack of professionalisation in the management infrastructure at all levels as an inevitable consequence of excessive officialisation" [pp. 184-85].

While the refrain of all committees and working groups had been that the co-operatives have not done as well as they should have, the experience of Commercial Banks and RPBs has shown that the weaknesses which were earlier considered at those peculiar to the co-operative system in fact arise from such deficiencies as relate to the structure of agricultural production itself [Para 5.10].

There are mainly two issues relating to the short-term co-operative credit structure which continue to be debated. One is about the size and viability of PACs and second with regard to the need for those-tier set-up. Apart from merits and demerits in each case, the view has been taken up till now by the policy-makers that, co-operative being democratic bodies, what is not acceptable to the cooperators should not be imposed on them. It is heartening to note that the recommendations of the Committee are quite pragmatic.

Numerically, in terms of membership, the co-operatives have spread widely in the country. By 1985-86, they covered 65 percent of the rural population. The ST and MT credit recorded an increase from Rs. 22 crore in 1950-51 to Rs. 3.140 crore in 1985-86, while the long-term credit increased from Rs. 12 crore in 1960-61 to Rs. 533 crore in 1985-86. Other areas in which co-operatives have made an indelible impression are fertiliser distribution, milk production, sugar production, cold storage and distribution of consumer goods [para 5.13]. However, while in some states like Punjab and Kerala, the system is strong, in many others it continues to operate at much below the desired level of expectation [Para 5.14]. It has been said of co-operation that it has failed in India because it has been both state sponsored and state patronised. With the excessive government intervention in the affairs of the co-operatives, effective non-official leadership along with democratic management disappeared altogether (Para 5.15).

The basic requirement of all the tiers working as a cohesive system is the mutuality of support among various tiers. Three must be a system of mutual accountability and obligations among the higher and the lower tiers. The higher tier should exercise an effective leadership role through an efficient system of supervision, training and management guidance by professionally skilled personnel. There must also be a commonly shared interest in deposit mobilisation and in profits and reserves [Para 5.17].

A major weakness of the co-operative system has been the neglect of the base level institutions and the tendency of the higher level institutions to look after their own interests often at the cost of the primaries. The co-operative credit system has woefully neglected its basic responsibility towards mobilising deposits, with the lower tiers looking up to the higher tiers for refinance at all levels [Report—Khusro Committee ,Para 5.22]. As many as 43-45 percent of PACs were in loss in 1984-85. The Report has stated that, "the PACs are even today not strong or efficient enough to discharge their responsibilities" [Para 224]. As regards DCCBs, 175 out of 352 banks are considered as week and inefficient banks. Despite the fact that "the percentage of deposits to Working Capital has shown an increasing trend to most of the states indicative of greater self reliance than in earlier years," high overdues have adversely affected their ability to avail of adequate refinance from higher tier agencies as the Committee says, "this has led to the chocking of credit lines and denial of financial assistance of agricultural members of Affiliated PACs" [P. 224.]

The powers which vest in the government under the co-operative law and rules are all-pervasive. Compounded further by their lack of self-reliance and their dependence on higher tiers and the government, the state has come to gain almost total financial and administrative control over the co-operatives, in the process stifling their growth. This trend must be reversed progressively, the powers which tie with the Registrar to-day should be vested in the higher tier organisations in respect of its lower tier [Paras 5.36 to 5.38] The Committee has asked for a "programmed effort" consisting of many oft-repeated measures, deposit mobilisation, augmenting share capital, etc., Apart from these, measures have also been suggested to improve loan procedures and policy including crop loan system, fixing of due date for recovery, normal credit statement, scales of finance and management of PACs. The Committee has suggested the need for "Primary Co-operative Development Fund" in DCCBs and SCBs recommended earlier by CRAFICARD.

There is no doubt that, for the realisation of all the improvements recommended by the Committee, while the country "recaptures the spirit of co-operation" and there is "an awareness among all the tiers of the system that such a functional relationship is needed for the development of the total organisation", equally important is the awareness on the part of political parties and government that Co-operative system cannot prosper under rigid state control. The Committee points out, some of the unhealthy results of politicisation are interference in the recovery of co-operative dues or promise to write off the dues if elected to power, and determination of interest rates on considerations other than financial returns, i.e., with an eye on populist appeal, such actions generate a general psychology of non-repayment, vitiating the recovery climate and jeopardising the financial interest of credit agencies. Paradoxically, state partnership which was conceived as an effective measure for strengthening the co-operative credit institution has paved the way for ever increasing state control over co-operatives, culminating in virtually depriving the co-operatives of their democratic and autonomous character. Effective non-official leadership alongwith democratic management has disappeared altogether. The time has come to reverse this process [Paras 5.40 to 5.45].

The essence or basic features of co-operative banking system must be a larger reliance on resources mobilised locally and a lesser and lesser dependence on higher credit institutions. Heavy dependence on outside funds has, on the one hand, made the members less vigilant, meet treating these funds as their own, and on the other, led to greater outside interference and control. Overall, this has made the co-operatives a mediocre, inefficient and static system [Paras 5.27 to 5.29].

The overdues problem of LDBs has become more serious over the years, even when their loans result in the creation of productive assets and should normally generate adequate incremental income to repay the loans. Though the Committee considers "the phenomenon of high overdues...more puzzling," the major damaging facts- to recovery, absence of fear of legal action leading to wilful default and lack of will among the borrowers to repay-are as clear as daylight. Among other causes of high overdues, the Report rightly says that to an extent, defective practices are at the root of the defaults, such as fixing of wrong repayment of schedule without proper correlation with the cash flows of the project, inadequate unit cost, not ensuring the availability of working capital, not granting reschedulement/rehabilitation facilities in the case of infructuous investments like failed wells, ineffective supervision over the end use of loans etc. [P. 306].

The issue of integration of short and long-term structures arose for the purpose of providing 'one contact point' to the farmers for getting all their credit needs and other allied services. The key to this integration is the contact point at the village level by the establishment of multipurpose farmers service societies. As the position stands today, the PACs have not emerged as efficient multipurpose societies and we have to agree with the Committee when it states that "it cannot...be said that conditions exist in which integration can now be attempted successfully" [P. 313]. "The question is also whether we should disturb the existing set-up for doubtful gains when integration is also not acceptable to those co-operators who are directly involved. What is more relevant at present, as the Committee puts, "is to ensure effective co-ordination between the two structures" [p. 314].

The net outcome of all the above factors has been to impart a great deal of inefficiency, high costs, how or negative profitability, inefficient service and lack of self-reliance in the co-operative organisations, especially at the level of the PACs. It is thus necessary that the country recaptives the spirit of co-operation, its culture, its discipline and above all its ethos. This can only be achieved with a cohesive structure based on a strong foundation at the primary level during inspiration from the higher tiers which are professionally managed under a dynamic and motivated leadership. But, evidently, the Committee did not think that the time had come to reverse the process of creating new institutions. It argued that the state apexes in the credit structure and the other larger co-operative banking systems with all-India jurisdiction have yet no national level bank of their own to function either as a national balancing centre of the surpluses of the state systems of the national level non-credit co-operative systems or the larger co-operative enterprises; these functions are today done in some areas perfunctorily and in others (such as deposit holders), effectively by the commercial banks. Only a national apex co-operative bank could fill the systematic gap and hopefully help to build the systematic strength and cohesiveness which sterns from a union of the state apexes. Hence, the Committee recommended the establishment of a National Co-operative Bank of India [CBI-RBI 1989, pp. 323-26, paras 8.01 to 8.09]. This is a proposal which required a much closer examination of the respective roles of NCBI and NABARD. Though the Committee as a whole has left NABARD untouched while recommending a separate national bank for the co-operative sector and considers that the new bank "will be of great assistance to NABARD in its vital role of institution building in the co-operative sector", there is lurking fear regarding (i) the overlap in some respects between NABARD and the new bank, (ii) to what extent the co-operative bodies would use to delink themselves from the commercial banks, and (iii) about the real scope from the success of such a bank, particularly when it is expected to "function on its own momentum distancing itself from government patronage with the concommitant government control and interference as well as props including financial support from it" [P. 336].

Present Structure and Growth

The co-operative credit structure has two features, namely, production credit (short-term credit structure) and investment credit (long-term credit structure). The short-term credit structure consists of Primary Agriculture Credit Societies (PACS) at the base level, District Central Co-operative Banks (DCCB) at the intermediate level and State Co-operative Banks (SCB) at the apex level. The DCCBs and SCBs are organised essentially as federations of primary societies. The long-term co-operative structure came into existence as Central Land Mortgage Banks in the twenties, primarily, as purveyors of credit for redemption of debt. It evolved over the years to meet investment credit needs of the farmers and later came to be known as State Land Development Banks (SLDBs), now known as State Co-operative Agriculture and Rural Development Banks (SCARDBs). They have either a unitary structure with branches in some states or a federal structure supporting the Primary Co-operative Agriculture and Rural Development Banks (PCARDBs) and their branches in the other states. Commercial Banks form another important constituent of the rural credit system purveying all types of loans: This is shown in Table 4.1.

Table 4.1 : Branch Network of RFIs

Institutions	*No. of Banks*		*No. of Branches*	
	1981	*1996*	*1981*	*1996*
Commercial Banks	85	94	28171	32200H
Regional Rural Banks	121	196	4795	14291H
Co-operative Banks Short term structure				
SCB	27	28	428	742
DCCB	337	363	7022	11663
PACS	-	-	94484	92682
Long-term structure				
SCARDB (Unitary structure)	8	8	1018	1172
SCARDB (Federal Structure) (PCARDBs)	12	11@	858	733
Total number of retail outlet			129326	141078
Number of villages/outlet			4.31	3.95
Rural population/outlet			3946	4824

@Excluding Andhra Pradesh where integrated (single window) structure is operating.

Source: EPW – October 18-24, 1997 – 'Geering Rural Credit for the, Twenty First Century. - K.P. Agarwal, V. Puhazhendhi and KTS Satyasaain.

The growth of grass roots level Rural Financial Institutions (RFIs) has been remarkable. The total number of PACS stood at 92,682 by end of March 1996 with a membership of around 966 lac. With the growth in the total number of retail outlets of all RFIs together, the combined figure worked out to 3.95 villages and about 5,000 of rural population for each outlet in 1996. There is some improvement compared to 1981 when there was only one outlet for 4.31 villages. To a considerable extent, the institutional agriculture credit structure has been somehow successful in piercing the stronghold of private money lenders and has also brought about some order in the attitude and functioning of private money lenders. In spite of an impressive expansion of the credit system, it is often felt inaccessible to the rural poor.

From an analysis of the rural credit system it appears that from time to time the system has been sought to be strengthened by reinforcing rural credit structure with new institutions. When co-operatives failed to cope up with rural problems, commercial banks were introduced and then to ensure equity in credit delivery RRBs were included and now came the proposal of private local area banks and linking with SHGs. It is, perhaps, rightly so because as Indian experience has shown that creating/involving new agencies has not helped much improve the prevailing system and in fact

Table 4.2: Flow and Stock of Short Term Loans by Agencies

	PACS		*RRBs*		*CBs*		*Total*	
	DISB	*OS*	*DISB*	*OS*	*DISB*	*OS*	*DISB*	*OS*
1973-74	691	807			105	179	796	985
1979-80	1260	1697			455	949	1714	2645
1982-83	1908	2225	98	109	565	1351	2571	3685
1984-85	2323	2836	132	206	1035	1964	3490	5006
1989-90	3974	4984	336	575	1898	4005	6208	9527
1991-92	4403	5816	337	679	2341	4631	7081	11126
1992-93	5575	7935	451	789	2432	4988	8458	13713
1993-94	5972	6640	476	887	2860	5425	9308	12952
1994-95	6903	7091	688	1115	3842	6154	11433	14360

Notes: Disb – Disbursement. OS-Outstandings.

Source: RBI. Report on Currency and Finance, Volume I. Various Issues + *EPW* – 18-24, 1997 – 'Gearing Rural Credit for the Twenty-First Century.'

such steps created new problems. For example, RRBs created to improve access of weaker sections to credit themselves became weak links in the credit structure and lot of energy is being spent in reviving them, Possibly the same objective could have been achieved by imposing control on the then existing agencies.

However, the flow of credit for agriculture and rural development gone up impressively over time. Total short-term credit flow rose from about Rs. 796 crore in 1973-74 to Rs. 11,432 crore in 1994-95. Correspondingly the outstanding amount rose from Rs. 985 crore to Rs. 14,360 during the same period (Table 4.2).

Table 4.3: Flow and Stock of Term Loans by agencies

	PACs		*RRBC*		*CBs*		*Total*	
	DISB	*OS*	*DISB*	*OS*	*DISB*	*OS*	*DISB*	*OS*
1973-74	229	1169			114	257	343	1420
1979-80	638	2153			520	1415	1158	3568
1982-83	809	2930	124	273	660	2792	1593	5995
1984-85	831	3531	178	490	1456	4649	2436	8670
1989-90	1433	5618	312	1263	2385	111279	4129	18160
1991-92	1863	7067	260	1306	2465	12351	4588	20723
1992-93	2089	7869	247	1343	2528	13300	4864	22512
1993-94	2445	8676	276	1673	2540	13688	5261	34037
1994-95	2506	8031	395	1894	3566	14766	6468	24691

Note: DSB- Disbursements: OS – outstandings.

Source: RBI, Report on Currency & Finance, Vol. 1, Various Issues. *EPW*, October 18-24, 1997, "Growing Rural Credet for the twenty first century. —K.P. Agarwal, V. Puhazhendhi and KTS Satyasai.

Short-term credit to agriculture grew at 13 percent during 1973-85 and showed a lower growth rate at 10.7 during the second period, i.e., 1986-94. Term credit flow presented somewhat better growth rate at 17.5 percent compared to short term credit flow in the first period though its performance in the second period was less impressive. The outstanding amounts for both short-term and term credit showed similar performance. The agency-wise growth rates reveal that commercial banks in general showed higher growth rates during the period 1973-85 in respect of short-term and term loans in terms of disbursements. In case of outstanding commercial banks showed markedly higher growth rates compared to co-operatives. Though RRBs showed higher growth, their growth is not strictly comparable as the growth rates are for the period 1982-85 only.

Table 4.4: Growth Rates of Flow and Stock of Short-term and Term Credit to Agriculture

Particulars	*Disbursements*		*Outstanding*	
	1973-85	*1986-94*	*1973-85*	*1986-94*
Short-term loans				
Co-operatives	10.8	10.6	12.1	9.9
Commercial Banks	19.1	10.6*	21.2	10.4*
RRBs@	14.8	12.9	31.9	14.8*
Total	13.0	10.7*	15.1	10.4*
Term loans Co-operatives	12.0	10.4	10.3	9.7
Commercial Banks	22.4	7.5*	26.7	9.8
RRBs@	18.0	3.7@	29.2	11.2*
Total	17.5	8.4*	16.7	9.9*

Notes: * Indicates that difference in the growth rates between two sub-periods is significant at less than or equal to 10 percent.

@ Growth rates for first period are for the years 1982-83 to 1985-86 only

Source: EPW-Oct. 18.24, 1997.

The shares of different agencies in the total short-term credit are presented in Table 4.5. Out of the total short-term credit disbursed, co-operatives that accounted for about 87 percent in 1973-74 now account for 60 percent in 1994-95. During this period, the share of commercial banks increased from 13 percent to 34 percent.

Thus by 1994-95 Co-operatives still have a major share in the disbursements of short-term credit. The share of co-operatives in oustanding credit is lower than their share in the disbursements. RRBs which enered the business in the mid-1970s, accounted for 6 percent of the disbursements and 7.8 percent of the outstanding amount by 1994-95 [Source –*EPW*, Oct 18-24, 1997.]

Table 4.5: Shares of Institutional Sources in Short-term Credit to Agriculture, 1973-94 (percentage)

	Disbursements			*Outstandings*		
Year	*CBs*	*Co-Ops.*	*RRBs*	*CBs*	*Co-Ops.*	*RRBs*
1973-74	13.24	86.76		18.12	81.88	
1979-80	26.52	73.48		35.87	64.13	
1982-83	21.97	74.22	3.81	36.66	60.39	2.95
1984-85	29.65	66.57	3.77	39.24	56.65	4.12
1989-90	30.57	64.02	5.41	42.03	51.93	6.03
1991-92	33.06	62.18	4.75	41.62	52.28	6.10
1992-93	28.75	65.92	5.33	36.38	57.87	5.76
1993-94	30.73	64.16	5.11	41.89	51.26	6.85
1994-95	33.60	60.38	6.02	42.86	49.38	7.76

Source: *EPW* Oct 18. 24.1997 = 'Gearing Rural Credit for the twenty-first century.'

The agency-wise shares in the term credit are given in Table 4.6. Commercial Banks emerged as major players in purveying term credit. They account for 55 percent of the disbursements in 1994-95 compared to their share of 33 percent in 1973-74. Co-operatives, on the other hand, account for 39 percent of the disbursements of term credit in 1994-95. In terms of outstanding credit the share of commercial banks increased from about 18 percent to about 60 percent during 1973-94. In the same period, share of Co-operatives declined from about 82 percent to about 33 percent. Thus, commercial banks and co-operatives have attained district market shares in terms of the type of credit. That is, commercial banks have major market share for their loans and co-operations for short-term loans.

Table 4.6: Shares of Institutional Sources in Term Credit to Agriculture 1973-94

(Percentage)

	Disbursements			Outstandings		
Year	*CBs*	*Co-Ops.*	*RRBs*	*CBs*	*Co-Ops.*	*RRBs*
1973-74	33.17	66.83		18.09	81.91	
1979-80	44.92	55.08		39.65	66.35	
1982-83	41.42	50.77	7.81	46.58	48.57	4.56
1984-83	41.42	50.77	7.81	46.58	48.57	4.56
1984-85	58.55	34.12	7.32	53.62	40.73	5.66
1989-90	57.75	34.70	7.55	62.11	30.94	6.96
1991-92	53.72	40.61	5.66	59.60	34.10	6.30
1992-93	51.98	42.95	5.08	59.08	34.96	5.97
1993-94	48.27	46.47	5.25	56.94	36.09	6.96
1994-95	55.14	38.75	6.11	59.80	32.53	7.67

The coverage of small farmers by the institutional sources, however, is not commensurate with the vast extension of the formal credit system in the country. This is shown in the Table below (Table 4.7). About 68 percent of the term credit from commercial banks was extended to farmers holding above 2 ha (5 acres). The restricted access of small farmers to co-operative credit is further highlighted by the fact that only 30 percent of the farmers holding less than 1 ha were members of PACCS whereas almost all the farmers holding above 4 ha are members of PACS. Though it was observed that the share of small farmers in the loans is higher compared to their share in the operated area, it can, however, not be construed as a favourable development for small farmers. For the impact of credit on small farmers is not satisfactory (RBI 1989). "Also, as rightly pointed out by Rao (1994), a large share of the loans to small farmers have been IPDP loans, and the data being at all-India level, is not true for majority of the states as indicated by the fact that southern states with a smaller average holding accounted for 52 percent of total loans. Thus, access of small farmers to institutional credit is restricted. Farmers holding above 2 ha of land have been dominating the co-operative membership and credit availment from the co-operatives as well as commercial banks. It is evident from field studies that marginal and small farmers are still dependent on non-institutional sources for as such as half of their credit needs". [EPW October 18-24, 1997 – Gearing Rural Credit for twenty-first century – p. 2723].

Table 4.7: Share of Small and Marginal Farmers in the Credit 1993-94

	Upto 5 Acres		*5 Acres & Above*		*Total*	
	No.	*Amt.*	*No.*	*Amt.*	*No.*	*Amt.*
Short-term Loans						
CBs	78.06	66.75	21.75	33.25	100.00	100.00
PACs	49.88	34.97	27.00	49.92	100.00@	100.00@
Term Loans						
CBs	72.60	32.35	27.90	68.24	100.00	100.00
PACs	56.99	46.62	43.01	53.37	100.00	100.00

Notes: @ Figures do not add up to 100 as distribution for some loans is not available.

Source: RBI, Report on currency and Finance, Vol. II, *EPW,* Oct- 18-24, 1997. 'Gearing Rural Credit for the twenty first Century'

"At the institutional level, the build up of overdue has severely restricted the capability of the rural financing institutions to recycle the funds and sustain the tempo of growth, and also impaired the eligibility of the credit agencies for availing of refinance facility from NABARD. This aspect has more relevance in the case of the RRBs and the co-operatives which heavily depend on NABARD for their lendable resources. Mounting overdue also result in increasing the transaction cost for effecting recovery. Aging of overdues has added further dimension to the problem as the overdues for more than three years have increased from Rs. 1,492 crore in 1986-87 to Rs. 2,842 crore in 1991-92, which constitute more than one-fourth of the total overdues [NABARD 1994]. This has happened despite the fact that a sizeable amount of overdues had been written off under the Agricultural and Rural Debt Relief Scheme. There is a widespread agreement in recent years that the problem of overdues has been aggravated because of short-sighted political interventions. Besides, the definiencies in loaning procedures of the rural financial institutions, especially those pertaining to appraisal, supervision and control, have also contributed to the malady of high overdues. A solution to this malady has been suggested by providing more autonomy to the lending institutions and at the same-time making them accountable for their financial results. Poor response to the crop insurance scheme and loss-making operations of the same, have also contributed to non-wilful defaults.

The overdue position of different rural financial institutions show that overdues have been an all-pervasive phenomenon across different agencies. Co-operatives are a shade better than RRBs and commercial banks in the recent years in terms of overdue rates (Table 4.8).

The downward trend in overdue percentage, however, should be taken with circumspection as the operation of ARDR (Agriculture and Rural Debt Relief) scheme seems to be responsible for it".

Source: Gearing Rural Credit for twenty-first century – *EPW* Oct. 18-24, 1997, pp. 2723-24].

Table 4.8: Proportion of Overdues to Demand Agency-wise

Agency	*1991*	*1992*	*1993*	*1994*	*1995*	*1996*
DCCBs	34	34	32	32	30	31
SLDBs	41	50	48	43	38	39
RRBs	55	60	59	54	49	39
CBs	42	46	44	44	43	-

Source: EPW – Oct 18-24, 1997 – 'Gearing Rural Credit for the twenty-first Century', p. 2725.

The Linear and Compound Growth Rates have been computed to study the trend in the growth of short-run, medium and long-term and total direct agricultural advances of co-operatives during the period 1960-61 to 1992-93 and the results are presented in Table 4.9.

Table 4.9: Linear and Compound Growth Rates of Co-operative Credit in India from 1968-69 to 1992-93

Co-operative Credit	*Linear growth*		*Compound growth*		
	Growth Rate %	*T. Value*	*Growth Rate %*	*T. Value*	*C.V%*
Short-term	35.7893	12.7450	10.4569	26.8453	67.9694
Medium & Long-term	126.1014	18.6742	11.1806	12.9076	63.3913
Total	44.2277	14.4203	10.5132	28.3923	66.4405

Source: Computed from RBI, Report on Currency and Finance: Various Issues.

The average annual linear growth rates for short-term, medium and long-term and total credit disbursed by co-operatives during the period 1968-69 to 1992-93 are 36 percent, 126 percent and 44 percent respectively. From the calculated 't' values, it can be understood that all the three types of credit disbursements are statistically significant.

Ninth Five-Year Plan and the Cooperatives

In the last few years, subsequent to the introduction of economic liberalisation, the scope and content of credit in the Agricultural Sector have undergone a significant change in terms of their demand and need. The creation of enormous potential for exports, post-harvest management and value addition have spurred the demand for high value crops. Encouragement to private/foreign investments in some of the agricultural sub-sectors, increased participation of DFIs and non-credit institutions in agri-rural activities is envisaged to bolster the existing credit support. Further, higher credit flow for capital formation and enhancement of production are essential to meet the demands in productivity. In addition, it is also necessary to take into account the problems faced by the ground level institutions in respect of credit dispensation.

Note: The facts and figures of this section are mostly taken from the article. "Gearing Rural Credit for the Twenty-First Century" – K.P. Agrawal, V. Pushazhendhi and KJS Satyasai in Economic and Political Weekly (EPW – Oct 18-24. 1997, pp. 2717-2724). For developing this chapter I am grateful to them and also to the journal. EPW.

In order to give shape to the tasks to be performed in the direction in the next five years, 'Working Group on Agricultural Credit and Co-operation' (including crop Insurance) was constituted by the Planning Commission on 12 December 1995 for projecting the credit requirements and suggesting strategic measures for strengthening the co-operative structure during the Ninth Five-Year Plan period. In view of the important role played by co-operatives in purveying Agricultural Credit, the Planning Commission has laid considerable emphasis for evolving strategies in the context of financial sector reforms on the specific problems of co-operatives and carrying out a greater role for them in the future.

In order to boost the production, the Agricultural Sector had received special consideration during the Eighth Plan period. Various strategies were evolved which envisaged increasing foodgrains production to meet domestic demand, diversification of agriculture including promotion of agro-based industries, creation of rural infrastructure and reinforcement of poverty all eviction programmes. A greater role has also been assigned to the private sector for a substantial step-up in investment in agriculture to the tune of Rs. 96,800 crores (Rs. 34,048 crores in Seventh Plan period), besides the investment in public sector with an allocation of Rs. 52,000 crores in the Eighth Plan outlay. The institutional credit has played an important role in increasing the agricultural production. The Co-operatives, Commercial Banks, and RRBs have been meeting substantially, the production/working capital needs as also those arising from investment credit requirements in the Agricultural Sector with the daunting task of meeting the credit needs on the one hand and maintaining their own financial health on the other.

In terms of the total credit flow, the share of co-operatives increased by 3.3% from 53.1 percent (Rs. 24095 crores) during Seventh Plan to 56.4 percent (Rs. 60977 crores) during Eighth Plan. It is interesting to note that the performance of the Co-operative Banks is expected to be better in terms of the level of achievement (123%) of the Working Group (WG) target for Eighth Plan while the same for CBs/RRBs has been of the order of 56%; although the overall achievement is expected to be 81%; Working Group points out, "(i) The overall position of credit flow in the Seventh and the Eighth Plan periods presents a mixed picture. The picture of credit expansion would have been different with the following attributes;

(a) The performance of CBs could have been better if the banks had reached the prescribed priority sector target fixed for agriculture lending.

(b) While the ARDR Scheme had initially dampened the flow of credit, the banks perhaps could have done better by more effective credit planning for supporting the viable/bankable projects/programmes with the infrastructure/linkage support from the State Governments.

(ii) The flow of credit during the Ninth Plan period under the priority sector is required to be expanded consistent with the projected demand. For the purpose, the strategies to be adopted are:

(a) diversification of agriculture both traditional/non-traditional areas with technology support,

(b) encouragement to the commercialisation if Agriculture (as agri-business) and agro-processing,

(c) expanding the traditional areas such as integrated land and water management, improvement in watershed development and rainfed farming,

(d) value addition for better return and employment generation,

(e) development of infrastructure, input distribution and linkages,

(f) promotion of research and extension,

(g) strengthening the rural credit delivery system, and

(h) expanding the deposit base of banks, particularly of the Co-operatives.

Concern about the paucity of resources to support the envisaged flow of credit, especially in regard to co-operatives, had been expressed while formulating the proposals for the Eighth Plan period. In this context suitable means of resource mobilisation for the LT Co-operatives (ARDBs) through instruments such as deposits, may have to be evolved. The National Bank for Agriculture and Rural Development (NABARD) has been providing, since its inception, consistently increased level of refinance support to augment the resources of the banking system."

The expected share of the various agencies in the disbursement of credit during the Ninth Plan period has been assessed by the Committee (1) keeping in view the average institutional share in credit flow during the Eighth Plan as also considering the health of such agencies and the sources available with them. Accordingly, the following agency-wise shares in credit flow have been considered by the Group.

Table 4.10

	Commercial Banks	*RRBs*	*Total (CBs+RRBs)*	*Cooperatives Structures*		*Total*
				ST	*LT*	
ST	32%	8%	40%	60%		60%
MT/LT	67	7%	74%	7%	19%	26%

Co-operative banks are expected to substantially fall short of the resources required for meeting their share of demand for credit (ranging from 7574 crores in 1997-98 to Rs. 15,950 crore in the year 2001-02). The likely resource gap in these institutions may be reduced with the refinance support from the NABARD, besides the mobilisation of additional resources from the market by way of deposits and borrowings.

In order to meet the emerging demand, adequate credit dispensation in time assumes greater importance. With a view to meeting the resource gap ranging from Rs. 9658 crore to Rs. 15,607 crore in the estimated credit flow of Rs. 229750 crore during the Plan period, the following measures, as suggested by the Working Group, are required;

(i) Capacity building of ARDBs, PACs and RRBs with legal mandate and financial assistance for cleaning their balance sheets alongwith organisational development, autonomy and transparency in operations.

(ii) In view of stronger relevance of and dependence on refinance from NABARD particularly for cooperatives, strengthening of NABARD with appropriate amendments in the legal framework increasing financial support and organisational re-engineering would be necessary.

(iii) Provision from Central Plan outlay to NABARD for development of rural infrastructures in public/government sector other than the co-operatives. This would supplement the efforts made through RIDF.

The tiered structure of the co-operatives was ingeniously designed to integrate them with the financial markets of the country on the one hand and their clientele at the village level on the other. A similar arrangement was also made available to the RRBs through their sponsor Banks. The institutional structure has an extensive reach, comprising, as of March 1995, 90, 983 PACs, 10775 branches of 364 DCCBs, 747 Primary Land Development Banks, 1153 units/branches of PLDBs, 1060 branches of SLDBs 14536 branches of 196 RRBs and 20472 rural branches of CBs. Besides, 28 SCBs and 19 SLDBs are providing support as apex institutions with a total spread of 41227 outlets (2/3rd belonging to co-operatives) as per Report of Task Force. The target works out to rural population of about 5000 for each outlet, through the co-operatives are member based institutions. A study conducted by NCUI has shown that practically all the villages and 67% of households are covered by co-operatives (342000) of various types having membership of 170 millions.

The cooperatives have been playing a significant role in providing agricultural credit. There has been a quantum jump in the total agricultural credit provided by the co-operatives and the commercial banks. However, the coverage share of agricultural loans disbursed by the cooperatives and RRBs have risen from 53% to 56% and 5.4% to 5.8% respectively, while the percentage in respect of the CBs has dipped from 41.5% to 38% during Seventh and Eighth Plan periods. The role of the cooperatives has, therefore, remained significant in Agricultural Credit.

The primary level institutions in the co-operative credit structure were characterised by a large number of weak and uneconomic societies, many of which had become moribund on account of heavy overdues and losses. In order to make these institutions financially healthy, the RBI and NABARD have taken several initiations to rehabilitate them.

(i) *Rehabilitation programme for weak DCCBs* – the rehabilitation programme for co-operatives initiated by RBI in1969-70 was sought to be given a new vigour in the mid-eighties by a special 12 point programme. The programme did not have asignificnat impact primarily on account of lack of financial support from State Governments.

(ii) *Rehabilitation of Ground Level Co-operative Institutions* – for development of selected PACS/LAMPS, a 3 year, 15 point programme was introduced in 1985-86 in sixteen project districts. As at the end of 31 December 1990, all the 417 PACS and 157 LAMPS covered under the programme which were provided with financial assistance as grant soft loan by NABARD had shown considerable progress.

(iii) *Rehabilitation of weak PLDBs* – A 10 point programme for rehabilitation of weak branches/units of LDBs introduced in January 1986 was operative till 31st March 1991.

In order to play a vital role in the emerging reformed environment in the Ninth Five-Year Plan, the cooperators need to have an appreciative perception of the principles of the co-operatives in agricultural development. It would be a greater challenge to change the character, nature and functioning of the co-operatives by letting them unshackle themselves from the firm grip of political interference, transform their functioning on viable terms and make them responsive to market forces. The co-operatives can no longer depend on concessions and government's assistance and have to stand on their own to become vibrant and efficient. Thus, they can provide better services with adequate and timely credit to the producers,

This signal would make the co-operatives more farmer-friendly.

The time has come for the co-operatives to launch into a new role with their own resource base, a new highway of efficiency, unity and cost effectiveness for reaping the hest of the market opportunities unveiled by the economic reforms and the new GATT agreement. The co-operatives in India have to draw an international experiences of their counterparts which play a leading role, particularly in Japan, South Korea, USA, China, Indonesia and Malaysia. In Japan, 'NOKYO' the agricultural co-operative banking system has the sixth largest deposits amongst the banks in the World. To meet the present challenges, effective measures are necessary to equip the cooperatives adequately to face the competitive environment for their survival and growth. Some of the measures suggested by the Task Forces have been endorsed and strongly advocated by the Working Group for further action:

(i) Reorganisation and Restructuring.

(ii) Corporatisation to infuse the such needed efficiency.

(iii) Strengthening the balance sheets and profit orientation.

(iv) Strategic alliance with corporate sector and joint sector.

(v) Reduction of Government's control and creation of role awareness among the employees in the changing environment.

(vi) Awareness among cooperators about the dysemi situation in the world and its redefined role.

(vii) Building leadership skills.

The financial sector reforms since 1992 have been mainly focused towards commercial baking institutions (including RRBs). The Co-operatives come under the jurisdiction of States and, therefore, little has been done by the Central Government insofar as institutional development of co-operatives is concerned. Some significant steps towards rural credit reforms which have so far been taken/ initiated, related to emphasising the need for the co-operative credit Reforms in the Union Budget for 1994-95, deregulation of interest rates for the credit cooperatives (subject to a floor rate of 12%) etc.

With a view to systematising the reform measures for the rural financial system, it is felt that the Ninth Plan document should clearly enunciate the scope, the objectives and the strategies for rural credit reforms. The success of any reform measures is directly linked to appropriate legal and policy framework and well planned strategies and towards this end, stronger emphasis needs to be laid on institution building and adoption of policies conducive to efficient market driven financial intermediation.

It is expected that the proposed 'National Policy on Co-operatives' will be finalised soon and operationalised so that democratic management with business development and higher efficiency of the co-operatives could be zealously resorted to and safeguarded by proving them with adequate legal and functional autonomy by way of timely conduct of elections, professionalisation of management, informing their financial health and providing scope for the conduct of timely audit by professional auditors. The Working Group has strongly advocated for expeditious enactment/ amendment to the Central and State Co-operative clauses on the recommendations of Choudhary Brahma Prakash Committee Report. The Department of Agriculture and Co-operative, Ministry of Agriculture, Government of India has already formulated a draft legislation for amending the Multi-State Co-operative Societies Act, 1984 on the lines of the recommendations of this Committee Report. The Working group further recommends that while revamping the rural credit system and changing the policies, government's control through RCs may be withdraw gradually. The governments may make it clear to the cooperative system that they would have to stand on their own strength without any government support. The Group feels that the proposed enactment and the policy measures will go a long way in revitalising the Co-operative Movement in the country and infuse it with the qualities of democratisation and professional management free from needless external controls. The Working Group also feels that the cooperatives should be strengthened to improve their ability to mobilise resources and rehabilitate in the context of reforms by bringing expeditious amendments to the Laws of the Central/State Governments in line with the recommendations of the Choudhary Brahma Prakash Committee.

In view of the substantial resource gap likely to be experienced by the co-operatives on the basis of demand-supply position of credit, definite strategies would be required to be adopted for the Ninth Plan period. NABARD has so far been providing adequate refinance support for investment credit. Of late, the growth of NABARD's refinance has dipped to about 1% only in 1996-97 on account of its resource crunch. Turning to the flow of institutional credit, the operations of NABARD were further crippled because of the withdrawal since 1992-93 of the concessional assistance given by RBI through its LTO Fund (Long-term operations). These funds generated out of the profits of RBI used to provide, on a continuing basis, resources of a sizeable magnitude at nominal cost to NABARD, on the basis of these funds, NABARD was able to extend medium and long-term assistance to agriculture and other rural development projects at concessional rates of interest. Under the reforms regime, RBI is channelling the bulk of its profits to government of India to bridge its budgetary deficit. This is the most retrograde step which provides one more example of diverting funds away from productive sectors to promote consumption by government. The earlier LTO facility is restored the better it would be for rural developmnt. Rural credit through the co-operatives (along with CBs/RRBs) would suffer in the process. There is a lurking fear that the co-operatives would not be able to enhance their business for viable operations which is being tried to be achieved through implementing DAPs (Development Action Plan). The huge resource gap would not be met if the Co-operatives were to mop up additional deposits for which organisational capacity building would be required. Therefore, the workable strategies to be followed in the Ninth Plan period, among others, would be-

(i) Equipping ST/LT Co-operatives for mobilising additional deposits through encouragement to depositors with incentives.

(ii) Deposit Insurance Scheme for PACS and LDBs.

(iii) Phased and slow reduction of dependence on NABARD

(iv) Strengthening the resources of NABARD

(v) Reduction of the SLR Requirement for Co-operative and RRBs.

(vi) Adequate measures for loan recovery.

(vii) Enlarging the capital base of Co-operatives by capital contribution and savings by member.

(viii) Making adequate provision for building resources.

(ix) Adequate allocation of General Line of Credit by RBI to NABARD for meeting the demand for ST Credit of Co-operatives/RRBs.

The co-operatives are burdened with mounting overdues and may continue to face the same in future. Concerted efforts for overcoming the chronic problem are to be made by all concerned on an urgent basis because overdues are not only eroding the profitability but also increasing the transaction cost in recovery of chronic dues. It has been noted with concern that measures such as waiver of loans have had an extreme debterious effect on the credit structure. Such steps have also vitiated the credit/recovery atmosphere and led the institutions, particularly the co-operative credit structure to become incapable of viable functioning. In fact, viable functioning of the credit delivery system will be the basic requisite criteria for enhancing credit flow and development of agriculture and rural areas. The cooperative banks are at present governed by the Co-operative Societies Act as well as BR Act (AACs). There is no clear cut delineation of regulatory powers under these laws and therefore, even in the areas of baking business, interference from the State Government is not uncommon. Bringing in appropriate amendment to the B.R. Act, 1949 to delineate clearly the powers of RCS/State Government and those of the RBI with a view to protecting the sanctity of norms relating to banking functions may be examined.

The Agricultural Sector is on the threshold of a new era, with export opportunities opening up. This will, however, required a much higher order of farm credit support and marketing effort. Would the co-operative leadership be able to galvanize the farming community to a new height of awareness, discipline and performance? The narrow self-seeking attitudes of the Co-operatives have to be replaced with a dynamic organisational vision for business excellence. The co-operative laws have to be amended to remove government control and to strengthen the hands of co-operative management. The new policy changes and the amendments to the Act/s could be made equally applicable to all the tiers of the credit and Non-Credit Co-operatives.

[*Note*: The facts and figures are sourced from Report of Working Group on Agriculture Credit and Co-operatives (including crop insurance) for the Formulation of Ninth Five Year Plan: [Planning Commission, G.O.I.].

5

The Regional Rural Banks (RRBs)

Regional Rural Banks are the youngest members of the family of rural credit institutions set up in India. They have been set up specially to meet the credit requirements of the weaker sections of the rural society, whose problems came into sharp focus after the State Governments enacted legislation in the mid-seventies, for discharging the debts from the non-institutional sources, of marginal farmers and scaling down the debts of the small farmers, etc. Given the rising demand for rural credit, and the need to replace money-lenders with institutional agencies, these existed scope for another agency. Besides the volume of credit required, spatial diversities and social complexities of rural life called for a multi-agency approach to rural credit and the need for a third financial agency in rural areas was keenly felt. This agency would combine the advantages of both the co-operatives and the commercial banks leaving out the disadvantages of both. This, then was the background in which the Working Group on Rural Banks headed by Narasimham recommended the setting up of RRBs in 1975. According to the Working Group, "What is needed is an institution which combines the local feel and familiarity with rural problems which the co-operatives possess and the degree of business organisation, business ability to mobilise deposits, access to central money markets and 'modernised' outlook which the commercial banks have." The law relating to RRBs was first promulgated as an ordinance on September 26, 1975 which was replaced by the RRB Act 1976.

The Working Group headed by Shri Narasimham had observed "the existing institutions, as they are presently structured would not be able to fill the regional and functional gaps in the rural credit institutional system, within a reasonable period of time, even with such adaptations, reorganisation and restructuring as may be considered" and added that, "In a country of the size and regional diversity as ours, no single pattern, be it commercial banking or co-operative credit, can be expected to meet all the emerging requirements in all areas. A degree of adaptation and improvisation is called for the range of institutional alternatives widened. It is in this context what we have come to the conclusion that a new type of institution is necessary." In sum, the RRBs were set up as institutions which would help feel regional and functional credit gaps, help develop the activities of the weaker sections, have a local feel and familiarity with local problems and better capacity to mobilise deposits and access to central money markets and a modern outlook.

A review of their performance during the last 20 years would, however, reveal that they were successful in fulfilling some of the basic objectives underlying their establishment. In particular, their contribution in opening branches at unbanked/underbanked rural centres and also in providing institutional agricultural credit to weaker sections for their productive endeavour are really remarkable. Another areas where the performance of RRBs is considered satisfactory is the lower cost of operations. Till recently, establishment and operational costs of RRB branches were no doubt relatively smaller than the rural branches of commercial banks.

Under branch expansion, 92% of the 14,574 branches of RRBs were opened in unbanked/underbanked rural centres. They have also helped in reducing the spatial gap that existed earlier, a large number of branches were opened by them in commercially backward states. As at the end of March 1992, 43.5% of all the rural branches in North Eastern Region, 49.4% in Central Region and 42.7% in Eastern Region were opened by RRBs. Commercial banks could not have embanked upon such a large expansion in branch network in rural areas in such a short span of time considering the cost factor and manpower requirements involved. Similarly, the average outstandings per loan account of RRBs is only Rs. 2,810 as against Rs. 6,730 for commercial banks (in respect of their agricultural advances). RRBs, as at the end of March 1992, had a total loan outstandings of Rs. 4,027 crore spread over 119 lakh borrowal accounts. It is to be credit of Regional Rural Banks that in almost all the districts in the country, the district administration depends upon these banks (perhaps due to their large branch network) to a significant extent for loaning under IRDP/SC Action Plan etc.

On the other hand, in areas of viability, mobilization of deposits and recovery, RRBs performance is not rated satisfactory. RRBs suffer from built in non-viability due to the limited area of their operation, restricted scope of lending (loaning confined to target group only) and administered interest rates (majority of loans granted at 11.5% and they pay interest on term deposits at 12.5 to 13%) leaving little or no operating margin. With the implementation of NIT Award equating RRB employees salary with sponsoring commercial bank employees, the operations of RRBs have totally gone overboard since 1991 and today it is reported that around 150 out of the 196 RRBs are incurring losses and in a majority of cases their net worth is wiped out. The accumulated losses of these RRBs is reported to be around Rs. 550 crore, as at the end of March 1992.

Viability of RRBs has engaged the attention of all the committees reviewed the functioning of RRBs. The Working Group on RRBs (Narasimham Committee-1975) observed, "Indeed the success of these banks should be judged as much by their efforts at expanding and extending the area of rural credit as by the conventional yard stick of profitability". Conceding that initially RRBs are bound to incur losses due to their main focus on social objectives and lack of scope for cross subsidisation, the Committee was optimistic that RRB will eventually turn the corner. In the words of the Committee "viability has also a time dimension. It is certainly not our suggestion that these banks should remain unviable for all times but we should be prepared for these banks operating at a loss in the initial years". In order to reduce losses of RRBs, sponsor banks were asked to bear the cost of deputing staff, providing training to RRB staff free of cost and also providing refinance at a cheaper cost. Even these steps have not, in any significant measure, helped improve the profitability of RRBs.

The Dantwala Committee (1977) which had the earliest opportunity to review the working of RRBs was also optimistic on the "potential viability of RRBs." The Committee observed, "The financial results of the working of some of these banks do show that RRBs have the potential and capability to attain financial viability and become a profit making institution at a level of business of about Rs. 3 crore which could be expected to be reached in about 3 to 4 years." It has been, however, proved later that this optimism was grossly misplaced and the assumptions made were far off the mark.

By the time Kelkar Committee (1986) revised the working of RRBs, their financial position had deteriorated to such an extent that 130 out of 173 RRBs had incurred losses. The Committee while correctly identifying factors responsible for the non-viability of RRBs, had confined itself to recommending for more sacrifices in the form of subsidies on the part of the sponsoring agencies—particularly sponsor banks – to reduce the losses of RRBs by increasing share capital, reducing interest rate on refinance, higher rate on funds kept for SLR, taking total responsibility for training arrangements in respect of RRB staff and deputing additional staff to take care of inspection and credit of RRB branches. However, some of the suggestions made by the Committee like deploying surplus funds of RRBs in Government securities, etc., for improving the viability have not been given effect to. Thus, till recently, it can be said that no major policy/structural changes were envisaged for improving the liability of RRBs. Dantwala Committee, however, should be given in credit for recommending as early a 1977 for a radical change in the lending policy of RRBs for attaining viability.

Khusro Committee

In August 1986, the RBI appointed Agricultural Credit Review Committee (Chairman A.M. Khusro) which submitted its report in August 1989 (RBI 1989). While the refrain of all previous Committees and working groups had been that the co-operatives have not done as well as they should have. The Khusro Committee (1989) points out that the experience of Commercial Banks and RRBs have shown that the weaknesses which were earlier considered as those peculiar to the Co-operative system in fact arise from such deficiencies in the rural credit system.

Partnered by GOI, State Government and Sponsor bank in the equity in the ratio 50: 15 : 35, these new banks were conceived as low cost district banks exclusively to meet the credit needs of the target group, i.e., small and marginal farmers, agriculture labourers, artisans and other rural residents of small means. Between 1975 and 1986 the RRBs increased their number from 6 to 194, their branches from 17 to 12,838 and districts covered from 12 to 351. During the same period, their deposits increased from Rs. 0.10 crore to Rs. 1,785 crore. Admittedly, the RRBs have achieved considerable degree of success in taking the banking services to the very remote areas which had hitherto remained unbanked, and making available institutional credit to the weaker sections in these area [Paras 4.00 to 4.14 Report.]

These indices of past progress, however, do not reveal the whole story. The various working groups on RRBs had brought out the deficiencies in their working and in particular their inability to operate on a viable basis. A closer look on their performance to evaluate their impact on the rural credit structure reveals that RRBs have developed some serious organisational problems. These critical areas relate to their steep decline in profitability, poor recoveries and problems relating to management and staff. This Committee recommended that RRBs, with certain modifications to enlarge their scope and coverage, should become an integral part of the rural credit system and the RRB pattern should be adopted for the break of rural credit business of banks. While the government decided to make RRBs an integral part of the rural credit set-up, the other suggestions to enlarge its scope were not accepted as it was felt that RRBs should remain exclusively as small man's bank. Later in 1979, CRAFICARD also revised the working of RRBs and recommended certain marginal changes but wanted them to remain predominantly for the service of weaker sections in the rural areas. The Kelkar Committee revised the working of RRBs in1986 but suggested only marginal modification without diluting the RRB concept as a small man's bank. A point to be noted in this connection is the while the CRAFICARD and Kelkar Committee did not want the concept of RRB to be diluted but to be retained as it is, with certain ameliorative measures to strengthen their position.

While the RRBs suffer from financial weakness and mounting losses, lack of staff motivation, poor quality of lending and overdues, the sponsor banks had passed on the back of serving the rural poor to the RRBs. The question is how can a bank which is weak in all aspects serve the weaker sections promptly and adequately? It is in this context the present Committee had to consider future of RRBs in the rural credit system. In the present Committee's view, the objective of service to the poor could be achieved only by self-sustaining credit institutions, "RRBs structured as they are, in our view, are not the institutions which could fulfil this function" [p. 144]. The Committee's findings have brought out clearly that the basic advantages—supplementing rather than supplanting the existing institutions, low cost of operations, local feel through locally recruited staff, better absorptive capacity for refinance compared with co-operatives – which the Narasimham group assumed about the RRBs in 1975 have not been realised. A part of the reason for the failure of RRBs is on account of external factors such as socio-political environment.

After examining various alternatives to strengthen the RRBs for enabling them to serve the rural poor more effectively, the expert group "found these alternatives to be unsatisfactory half-way houses which do not solve the problem of service to the rural poor" and concluded that there is "no place for RRBs in the country's rural credit system of the future" [p 149]. Having rightly concluded that the RRBs have no future because of 'in-built non-viability' and other inherent weaknesses and converting RRBs into subsidiaries of their sponsor banks is 'self-defeating in purpose,' the Committee has recommended the merger of RRBs with their respective sponsor banks. Based on unrealistic assumptions under Indian conditions, the establishment of RRBs was a costly mistake and the sooner we rectify the mistake, the better it is for the banking system and for the benefit of weaker sections. What is needed now is that we should not stop with the merger of RRBs in sponsor banks but also go ahead for the merger of other commercial banks' rural branches in each district with the lead (sponsor) bank so that not only one single commercial bank for the rural areas in each district is strengthened but also the rural having system is simplified to the maximum extent, banking infrastructure costs are reduced and bank's ability to ensure better quality of loaning is improved. The Committee however, has suggested strengthening of one commercial bank having the largest number of branches for each block. Perhaps the need for more than one alternative source of credit in the rural areas in unduly over-emphasised or the committees unduly alarmed of the administrative problems involved in the merger/transfer/shifting of rural branches of other banks in each district.

Thus a stage has now come when a view has to be taken regarding the future set-up of RRBs especially in the present context of reforms envisaged in the financial sector. It is estimated that RRBs in the present set-up incur losses of about Rs. 50 lakhs per day. An overall analysis of their performance reveal that RRBs have fulfilled some of the basic objectives for which they were established and in the context of mounting losses incurred by them there is no case for continuing them in the present form for the reasons mentioned above.

Co-operative financial institutions and Regional Rural Banks (RRBs) contribute about 55 percent and 5 percent of total institutional credit to the rural poor. These institutions suffer from large loan defaults and a virtual erosion of repayment ethics. This has hampered recycling of resources and affected the very viability of institutions. For instance, in the case of RRBs a majority of the total 196 are deemed non-viable. In 1994-95 only 32 RRBs recorded profits while the remaining 164 posted a loss aggregating Rs. 420 crore. Reconstituting a dozen or so RRBs, or signing of memoranda of understanding (MOUs) with co-operative institutions can, at best, be regarded as an apology for action.

The Narasimham Committee Report on the financial systems

(1991) also dealt with the viability of RRBs and with a view to improve their profitability suggested enlargement in the scope of their lending to include financing bigger borrowers and bringing their interest rate structure to be in line with commercial banks. The Committee also recommended higher return on surplus funds of RRBs. Dealing with the future set up of RRBs, the Committee suggested that it could be left to the RRBs and sponsor banks concerned, whether the former could retain their individual identity or merge with sponsor banks' 'rural subsidiaries' (formation of which was recommended by the Committee). It has suggested that in the latter case, RRBs can be taken over as subsidiary of the sponsor bank to begin with. The Committee's suggestion for merging RRBs with the proposed 'rural subsidiaries has certain inherent advantages, but it cannot be implemented immediately as the proposal for commercial banks' creating rural subsidiaries' has not yet been examined and accepted by the Government of India. Further, the financial viability of such subsidiaries also is suspect as the basic feature of low returns available on agricultural lending will continue to be present. Further, how to absorb the existing accumulated losses and other liabilities of the RRBs and its impact on the working of the proposed subsidiary is an area of concern. This may again pose serious financial strain on the subsidiary and hence appears to be not feasible.

Broad Policies

This critical survey of the origin, growth and achievements of RRBs and also the problems faced by them, throws up various policy issues which call for a positive and dispassionate consideration.

The basic and fundamental policy question which requires an answer is whether we would recognise the role of RRBs in the rural credit system of the country and whether these institutions should continue as an important part of rural credit delivery system. It is well known that RRBs were introduced with the specific objectives of serving certain categories of rural people levelled as 'weaker sections' and that these institutions were structured to serve this objective. Dantwala Committee, reporting on RRBs in 1977, observed that this institutional innovation was well conceived and was necessary to make good some of the inadequacies in the existing rural credit system. The Dantwala Committee which studied the problem of the RRBs in 1977-78, has very lucidly explained this problem, "As for the RRBs... their major responsibility is to make available adequate and timely credit to the class of borrowers who for each of such facility are entirely at the mercy of private money lenders who often charge them exhorbitant rates of interest. This task, if it is to be effectively performed, would involve considerable extension work which would include such varied tasks as identification of projects which would help augmenting their incomes, assistance in the preparation of bankable projects, typing up arrangements for supply of inputs as also for marketing of finished products, and supervision over expenditure incurred...While we fully endorse the proposition that the weaker sections of the rural community should receive preferential treatment from the credit institutions, in our view, the purpose will be better served by direct assistance by the institutional agencies and the state Government in the form of intensified extension service for improving the production and productivity of the weaker sections, rather than by the system of differential rates of interest", [Report –Para 649, page 81].

This view received further support from the Kelkar Committee (1986) which observed that RRBs, as part of the multi-agency approach to rural credit, are particularly suitable to do the job envisaged for them. That as distinct level organisations, they can be trusted to take banking closer to rural people and the RRBs can exist side by side with co-operatives, and Commercial Banks, playing a supplementary role. After a detailed review of the working of the RRBs, the Kelkar Committee came to the fundamental conclusion that "... in view of its large branch network, comparatively lower cost of operation, local involvement through appropriate staffing pattern, and their operations more in tune with the national objective of serving the weaker sections comprising of small and marginal farms, artisans, village and cottage industries, RRBs as a part of the multi-agency approach to rural credit are eminently suitable to do the job envisaged for them. Further, as district level organisations they can be trusted to take banking closer to the rural households and ensure effective supervision over the end-use of credit." [Report, page, 6, para 2].

An important aspect of the role of RRBs in rural development which has not received sufficient attention, is that they are a powerful instrument of primary income distribution in the rural areas. Equitable income distribution can be direct or indirect and given the failure of the indirect method, direct method of income distribution become imperative, and RRBs have become a suitable instrument for bringing about equitable income distribution. This role of RRBs cannot be lost sight of, given the national objective of development with social justice. Therefore, both as a factor in the multi-agency approach to rural credit structure and as an instrument of income distribution in rural areas, RRBs have an important role to play in rural development. RRBs are not just rural credit agencies. They are more than that; they are a fruitful exercise in bank-led rural growth.

It cannot be denied that a rural credit institution has necessarily to be viable, particularly a credit institution designed to serve the weaker sections. To improve the viability, operational efficiency and managerial effectiveness of RRBs, the Kelkar Committee has made a number of recommendations, the most important is the viability. RRBs should not finance bigger borrowers and should retain their present image of a small man's bank. The loans should be advanced for the ultimate benefit of the borrowers falling in the target group of the RRBs—particularly in the area of operation of the RRB, so that the sense of local feel in the operations is not allowed to be diluted. The Committee's specific suggestions to improve the viability of RRBs are:

(a) provision of additional cost-free funds by way of increased paid-up capital of each RRBs from Rs. 25 lac to Rs. 100 lac, (b) lowering of involvement of sponsor books in RRBs loans, by reducing their refinancing of short-term loans from 30% to 20% accompanied by a reduction in the rate of interest from 8.5% to 7% per annum, (c) a judicious re-adjustment of loan portfolio by the RRBs to correct the mismatch between investment credit and working capital loans: RRBs cannot afford to be weak; it has to break even and become viable in the long run. But the question is whether the concept of viability of RRBs could be the same as the concept of viability of a commercial or business unit. The

RRBs are not given freedom in many of their affairs like the commercial banks; even its clientele is specific, scattered, remote and not assisted by anyone. Viability of RRBs needs to be assessed in terms of increasing socio-economic gains for their clientele. Viability of RRBs will have to be considered in terms of increase in business per branch, recovery rate, productivity of staff, cost-effectiveness of operations, closer monitoring and socio-economic upliftment and improvement in the standards of living of the clientele.

The Khusro Committee seems to have persuaded itself so much in favour of merger of RRBs that it has not thought it fit even to consider other alternatives which are workable. To argue for merger would amount to; removing an institution from the rural scene which has become really a small man's bank; putting the clock of rural progress bank; accepting the trickle-down theory and missing the fundamental point that RRBs have become an instrument of primary income distribution in the rural areas. In the ultimate analysis, it has to be borne in mind that the RRBs are expected to be not a 'transient or temporary structure' but a permanent set-up in the over-all rural credit superstructure of the country. Their financing and operations must be so organised as to ensure long-term viability. Any measure to tackle the problem with short-term solutions is not likely to be much helpful.

To sum up, the debut of Rural Banks in rural India—is helping to dynamise the rural economy. With the government's determined efforts to liquidate rural indebtedness, the traditional sources of credit are fast drying up. The setting up of RRBs provides an alternative source of effective credit supply to the small and marginal farmers, rural artisans and landless labourers. Moreover, the operations of the RRBs in the country, far from disturbing the Lead Bank Scheme, it is fact, helping the process of the fulfilment of the Lead Bank's dominant role in the particular area allotted to it. In short, the functions of the Lead Bank and the RRBs are not contradictory but complementary. Each is helping the other in the fulfillment of the different aspects of the District Credit Plan.

Table 5.1: Statement and Regional Rural Banks (as at the end of March 1996)

(Amount in Rupees Crore)

State	No. of RRBs	No. of Districts covered	No. of Branches	Deposits		Outstanding Advances						Advances Overdue	
						Direct		Indirect		Total			
				No. of accounts	Amounts	No. of accounts	Amounts	No. of accounts	Amounts	No. of accounts	Amounts	No. of accounts	Amounts
1	2	3	4	5	6	7	8	9	10	11	12	13	14
West Bengal	9	19	804	28,13438	969.8	12,37,795	455.7	5,040	5.7	12,42,835	461.4	6,65,961	166.6
Total All India	196	427	14497	388,57716	14,187.9	126,43,295	7470.5	16,070	34.5	126,95,365	7505.0	58,81,424	1,928.3

Source: National Bank for Agriculture and Rural Development

6

Micro Finance – The New Development Paradigm

The incapacity or disinterest of the formal banking sector to service the needs of low income clientele has become quite apparent by now. Earlier studies and surveys like AIDIS have established that institutional credit has not penetrated to the lower rungs of income and asset hierarchy, may be for robust economic reasons. This was true even of cooperatives, where small farmers face restrictions in becoming members. The formal sector's thrust even within the priority sector lending framework has been on productive activities, whereas the poor (large majority of whom are landless and non-cultivators) need credit mainly for financing income consumption gap or tiding over occasional crisis and emergencies. Obviously, the needs, and the terms and modes of delivery do not match. This could well be the reason for the increased dependence of rural people, more markedly of the non-cultivators, on informal credit sources like traders, contractors and moneylenders.

Given these, how can the gap between demand and supply of funds in the lower rungs of the rural economy be bridged? What mechanism (s) could be used for this? A tacit consensus appears to be shaping up, at least among the banking authorities and development professionals, that development agencies in the non-governmental sector should be called upon to act as the intermediaries in delivery and management of rural credit. Interestingly, the formal sector took the initiative to develop a supplementary credit delivery machanism by encouraging institutional arrangements outside the financial system (like NGOs) to act facilitators or intermediaries. The beginning was made in India with NABARD's pilot project in Karnataka (1991-92) of linking self-help groups with financial banks, mediated through the NGO Mysore Resettlement and Development Agency etc. This project, known as the *Bank-SHG Linkage Project*, was expected to the advantageous to the banking sector from the angles of both fulfilment of its social goals (like reaching out to the poor) and achieving operational efficiency (by externalising part of the transaction cost).

There has been a growing interest in the recent past in micro-finance, particularly in the context of reaching out to the world's poorest families. The interest reached its peak with the Micro Credit Summit held in February, 1997. This has initiated the process of ensuring delivery of credit for self-employment and development of micro-enterprises. The target is to reach 100 million of the world's poorest families especially the women. Micro credit has been defined in the Summit as 'programme that provide credit for self-employment and other financial and business services to very poor persons'. Micro finance is a wider term and refer to small-scale financial services provided to weaker sections of people particularly in the rural areas who work in agriculture, animal husbandry, fishing, household industries, crafts and small business.

Group-based models of micro finance have captured the attention of the development practitioners all over the world particularly after the success of Bangladesh Gramin Bank to reach out to millions of poor women. Even the most conservative development practioners cannot but take note of the rapid pace of expansion in the outreach of micro-finance institutions, mostly functioning outside the formal channels of credit delivery. By end 2003 about 80 million clients across the world were being serviced by approximately 2,900 such institutions (Table 6.1). India's share in the global micro-credit market in 2003 was 13 percent of all clients and 16 per cent of the poorest clients, thanks to the SHG linkage programme of the National Bank for Agriculture and Rural Development (NABARD). India, thus, is home to one of the largest micro-credit/ micro-finance programmes in the world.

Table 6.1: Global Outreach of Micro-credit, 1997-2003

Year	*No. of Reporting Inst.*	*Number of Clients Reached (Million)*	*Poorest Clients Reached (Per cent)*
1998	925	20.9	56.3
2000	1567	30.7	62.9
2002	2572	67.6	61.7
2003	2931	80.9	67.7

Source: Morduch 2004, Daley-Harris 2004.

Worldwise, the awareness of the importance of microfinance as a poverty reduction strategy, has been growing over the years. For about two decades, various experiments have been made to enhance to access of the poor to credit facilities in different countries both by the government as well as by the non-government organisations. Two different approaches have been identified in the development of the microfinance industry. The Latin American model that may be called the 'commercial model' has recognised from the outset the significance of staying with the formal financial system rather than contributors. There is an accent instead on enterprise creation and growth. The South Asian model, largely drawing on the strategic and operational features of the '*Grameen Model*', has its a spotlight clearly on women and poverty.

To some extent, micro-credit is not a new concept in India. Priority sector credit in general and weaker section credit in particular was actually a kind of micro-credit. In the 1990s during the banking sector reforms the definition of priority sector reforms underwent a sea change. So far as micro-saving services are concerned, these are indeed recent with the advent of self-help group (SHG) movement. Micro-insurance, however, is still in experimental stage. 'Micro-savings' has been a proxy for 'micro-insurance'. It is only the savings and credit aspects of micro-finance that have, therefore, been addressed so far in India.

In India, the banking industry has grown under two different systems of patronage. While the SHG linkage programme anchored by NABARD has the patronage of the government and other formal banking institutions, a parallel system promoted by non-statal agencies has been depending almost exclusively on subsidised external grants to finance both social mobilisation and onlending. Both target the poor and women, predominantly. Though there are no comprehensive estimates available on the outreach of the micro-finance sector to the poor, evidence suggests that about 80 per cent of the clients are without any formal savings, and 91 per cent, without formal credit. Nearly 77 per cent of the clients are in the rural sector.

In India where poverty still remains a major problem with about 320 million people forming 36% of the population living below the poverty line, NGO recognised micro-finance as one of the tools to attack poverty. They took to self-help group approach promoting people's organisations and functioning as feeder-banks linked under-reached and under served rural poor. They have facilitated the organisation of self-help groups for a common cause through a process of social mobilisation with varying entry points like removal of illiteracy, basic health care, access to local resources, removal of social ills, resolution of social conflict, protection of environment, thrift and credit, The old paradigm of micro-finance envisaged providing credit to poor people at subsidised rates through public and state owned banks of financial institutions. There is a significant departure in testing micro-finance innovations as alternative channel and depending on the prospects and potential, synerigise the tested approach with the formal system.

Micro-finance programmes are important institutional devices for providing small credit to the rural poor in order to alleviate poverty. Micro-financing programmes through SHGs, introduced and expanded by non-governmental organisations (NGOs) in several parts of India, have the potential to minimise the problem of inadequate access of banking services to the poor. A study by NABARD, which covered 560 SHG member households from 223 SHGs across 11 states, showed many positive results on the impact of participation of rural poor in the SHGs. It shows that there have been perceptible and wholesome changes in the living standards of SHG members in terms of ownership of assets, borrowing capacities, income generating activities, income-levels and increasing savings.

Since most of the SHGs are linked to formal banks for their deposit and loan mobilisation, it is a researchable issue, as to whether the informal micro-finance intervention through SHGs has had any impact on the deposit and credit accounts in the formal banks. With this backdrop, it requires a rigorous study to examine the association between operation of SHGs and formal banking habits, especially among the females. In the process, it traces out the socio-economic factors that determine individual and household formal banking habits and analyses the impact of SHG operation on individual and household banking habits. Studies of rural credit patterns reveal that a bulk of the loans sanctioned still go towards financing the income-consumption gap of the poor for expenses related to health and other exigencies, i.e., unproductive expenditure. The interest of private commercial banks in micro-finance is likely to yield a range of financial products in addition to credit facilities, which was the primary service delivered through NGOs. These include insurance policies (home, personal accidents and even weather insurance) to cover unforeseen events, as well as derivatives enabling farmers or traders to lock in futures are or purchase prices for commodities, thereby guaranteeing returns. Thus a whole range of essential financial services in rural areas are foreseen, with some important caveats, however. It is usually the rich, landed classes which are quick to avail of new opportunities and it is easy for relatively weaker sections of society, such as dalits, single women, the extremely poor or uneducated to be excluded, by default if not design. The new challenges for private commercial banks in the area of micro-finance is to ensure credit access to these latter sections..

The Reserve Bank of India (RBI), in its Report of the Internal Group on Rural Credit and micro-finance released in the month of July, 2005, highlighted how direct financing by banks have failed to penetrate the rural areas. Small loan amounts, high transaction costs of a large number of small accounts, 'unbankability' of borrowers and lack of collateral security have made banking in rural areas largely unfeasible. The SHG-Bank Linkage Model has been able to completely alter the socio-economic face of rural India. While the RBI report recommended banking correspondents and banking facilitators as agents for delivering banking services to remote areas, the tried and tested model of linking banks to self-help groups (SHGs) remains a way to bridge the gap between banks and the rural populace. Today, the success of this model can be gauged from the quantum jump in the number of SHGs being linked to banks every year. From 255 in March 1993 to 4,800 in March 1996, some 16 lakh SHGs have been linked to banks by March 2005. the figures for June show another 21,000 SHGs being linked to banks in the first three quarters of this financial year.

If the key indicators of success of a micro-finance programme are outreach and financial sustainability, then, on both these parameters, the SHG-Bank Linkage Model can be called a great success. It is true that while, on the one hand, the number of SHG-linked banks in geometric progression, the model provides a win-win situation for both banks and the SHGs. SHGs are a group of around 15 individuals who pool their savings into a fund from which they can borrow as and when necessary. Over time, they begin to maintain a group account with a bank and when the bank becomes convinced of its performance in generating savings, it starts lending to the group as a unit. The programme is financially viable for banks as their transaction costs are lowered and with close to 98% loan recovery. Savings of the group constitute the collateral with peer pressure within the SHG ensuring full recovery.

According to the NABARD, not only does the model help provide cheaper credit, it also completely changes the socio-economic conditions of the members for the better. About 90% of the SHG members are women. The number of SHGs linked to banks rose by over 300% since 2002 to reach nearly 7 lakh by June 2005. It is hoped that our next step is to develop the matured SHGs into micro enterprises by sharpening their skills for higher earnings in the future. While the programme is doing well, it still has a long way to go before making a big dent in rural areas. An NSSO survey showed that so far SHGs have reached only around 4.8% of farmer households in the country. This is shown in the Table 6.2.

Table 6.2

	Performance of Self-help Groups		
	March 1993	*March 1996*	*March 2005*
No of SHGs linked	255	4,757	1,525,243
% of women groups	70	74	90
Families assisted	5,100	80,000	19,830,000
Participating banks	14	95	560
NGO partners	32	127	3000
Districts covered	26	157	563
Aggregate bank loans	(Rs. Cr. 0. 29	6.06	6249

NABARD

CONCLUSIONS

The philosophical base for financial sector reforms is derived from macro-economic perspective along ignoring the micro-economics of development which is at the heart of micro-finance. The investigation into micro-economics of development has led, in the recent years, the elaboration of what is called institutional economics which takes a bottom up approach to economic development and reform. The central themes of the New Institutional Economic are transaction costs, information costs, and theory of collective action.

It is clear that micro-finance function has been the backbone of rural and semi-urban areas for the banking system and innovations are required on the lines suggested in the specific context of loan policy and procedures, transparency norms, flexible banking hours, etc. If one was to focus on 95 per cent of the borrowal account with the overall objectives of improving micro-finance activity, as per the goals set, we must have clearly segmented structures in the form of rural subsidiaries of commercial banks for carrying out innovations.

The optimistic vision of the Task Force to 'empower' 75 lakh poor households through strong and viable people's structures like SHGs and MFIs. It has to be seen in the light of these concerns. Behind this optimism lies hidden the long, chequred history of development in this country, which has shown scant respect for the interests and concerns of the poor, by not adhesive basic needs of the rural sector like land reforms, development of land and irrigation, marketing and transport infrastructure, etc. Credit is an important part of these, but not so overwhelmingly important than other urgent needs, like public investment in agricultural sector, especially in irrigation, are pushed to the background. Even credit will not be able to play its part in the long run, if investments are not made in developing rural infrastructure. Also, the innovative financial institutions being evolved at the grass roots would find it nearly impossible to carry out their business of lending to the poor on a sustainable basis.

Appendix

Table A.1: Banking Development After Bank Nationalisation

State Union Territory	June 1969			March 1997		
	Branches (Number)	*Deposits (Rs. Cr.)*	*Advances (Rs. Cr.)*	*Branches (Number*	*Deposits (Rs. Cr)*	*Advances (Rs. Cr.)*
1	*2*	*3*	*4*	*5*	*6*	*7*
1. Andhra Pradesh	567	163	147	4912	25850	20061
2. Assam	88	34	14	1238	5084	1789
3. Arunachal Pradesh	-	-	-	68	394	42
4. Bihar	272	169	52	4952	21222	6467
5. Delhi	274	449	291	1236	48847	32676
6. Goa	85	49	20	280	3834	957
7. Gujarat	753	402	195	3518	29059	14449
8. Haryana	171	53	26	1378	10354	4422
9. Himachal Pradesh	42	14	4	761	3676	861
10. Jammu and Kashmir	35	29	5	795	4717	1829
11. Karnataka	755	237	175	4509	26357	18842
12. Kerala	548	152	99	3123	22995	10783
13. Madhya Pradesh	343	111	65	4443	18127	9486
14. Maharashtra	1114	1125	1071	5969	101954	69998
15. Manipur	2	1	-	65	264	152
16. Meghalaya	7	9	3	179	892	127
17. Mizoram	-	-	-	78	285	40
18. Nagaland	2	1	-	71	490	118
19. Orissa	100	31	17	2160	7155	3504

20 Punjab	345	203	58	2349	23043	9015
21 Rajasthan	364	85	44	3239	14055	6215
22. Sikkim	-	-	-	42	240	42
23. Tamil Nadu	1060	294	381	4628	32487	32597
24. Tripura	5	4	-	180	694	262
25. Uttar Pradesh	738	365	173	8751	48304	15268
26. West Bengal	503	644	700	4312	36450	18241
UNION TERRITORY						
1. Andaman & Nicobar	1	-	-	31	189	30
2. Chandigarh	21	36	65	146	4061	3574
3. Dadra & Nagar Haveli	-	-	-	7	82	15
4. Lakshadweep	-	-	-	9	31	3
5. Pondicherry	12	5	5	74	831	324
6. Daman & Diu	-	-	-	13	206	45
All India	8187	4665	3610	63536	492227	282238

Source: Banking Statistics, Reserve Bank of India.

Table A.2: Branch Expansion

Population Group of Branches	*June 1969 (Number)*	*March 1997 (Number)*	*Increase (Number)*
Rural	1832 (22.2)	33008 (52.0)	31176
Semi-urban	3322 (40.2)	13641 (21.5)	10319
Urban	1447 (17.5)	9298 (14.5)	7851
Metropolitan	1661 (20.0)	7587 (12.0)	5926
Total	8262 (100.0)	63534 (100.0)	55272

Note: Figures in parentheses indicate percentage share in the total.

Source: Banking Statistics, RBI: Bombay.

Table A.3

Population Group of Branches	*June 1969 (Rs. Cr.)*	*March 1997 (Rs. Cr.)*	*Growth (Rs. Cr.)*
Rural	145	72511	72366
	(3.1)	(14.9)	(14.8)
Semi-Urban	1024	96658	95634
	(22.0)	(19.5)	(19.7)
Urban	1209	110292	109083
	(25.9)	(22.4)	(22.3)
Metropolitan	2287	212766	210479
	(49.0)	(43.2)	(43.2)
Total	4665	492227	487562
	(100.0)	(100.0)	(100.0)

Figures in brackets indicate percentage share in the total.

Source: Banking Statistics published by RBI.

Table A.4: Credit Expansion

Population Group of Branch	*Advances (Rs. Cr.)*		*CD Ratio (%)*	
	June 1969	*March 1997*	*June 1969*	*March 1997*
Rural	54	32372	37.2	44.6
	(1.5)	(11.5)		
Semi-urban	407	37478	39.7	38.8
	(11.3)	(13.3)		
Urban	722	51300	59.7	46.5
	(20.0)	(18.2)		
Metropolitan	2426	161088	106.0	75.7
	(67.2)	(57.0)		
Total	3609	282238	77.3	57.3
	(100.0)	(100.0)		

Figure in brackets indicates percentage share in the total.

Source: Banking Statistics: Reserve Bank of India.

Table A. 5: Sectoral Deployment of Credit

Sectors	*June 1972 (Rs. Cr.)*	*March 1996 (Rs. CR.)*	*Increase (Rs. Cr.)*
Agriculture	245	27085	26840
Small Scale Industry	639	31884	31245
Other Priority Sector Advances	93	14422	14329
Total Priority Sector Advances	977	73391	72414
Medium and Large Industries	2413	93108	90695
Wholesale Trade	1253	11993	10740
Export	NA	29692	29692
Others	657	23513	22856
Total	5300	231687	226397

Source: RBI: Annual Reports

Table A.6: Indian Banking : Then and Now

Indicators	*1974*	*1997*
Deposits (Rs. Crores)	1164	492227
Advances (Rs. Crores)	531	282237
Investments (Rs. Crore)	428	191091
Branches (Number)	4288	63534
Per Branch Deposits (Rs. crore)	0.27	7.75
Per Branch Advances (Rs. crore)	0.12	4.45
Per Capita Deposits (Rs.)	32	5237
Per Capita Advances (Rs.)	14	3002
Per Branch Population (in 000's)	82	15

Bibliography

Agarwal, K.P.V. Puhazhendhi and KTS Satyasai (1997), 'Gearing Rural Credit for the Twenty-first Century', *Economic and Political Weekly*, Vol. 32, No. 42, pp. 2717-28.

Ajit, D and R.D. Bangar (1998), 'The Role and Performance of Private Sector Banks in India (1991-92 to 1996-97)', *Political Economy, Journal of India 7*, and 2, 7-20.

Analyst (1993), 'Myth of Non-viability of Rural Branches', *Economic and Political Weekly*, Vol. 28(8), May 1, pp. 853-94.

Bauer, E.M., *International Conference on Agricultural and Co-operative Credit*, Vol. 2, 1952.

Bellshaw, *Agricultural Credit in Economically Underdeveloped Countries.*

Bhaduri, A, (1983), *The Economic Structure of Backward Agriculture*, Macmillan India Ltd.

——, (edited), *Studies in Rural Participation.*

Brinegar, G.K. & Fetting, L.P. *Some Measures of the Quality of Agriculture Credit*, NBER, N.Y. 1968.

Capstick, Margaret, *Economics of Agriculture*; George Allen & Unwin, 1970.

Caternach, I.J., *Rural Credit in Western India*, 1875-1930, O.U.P. 1970.

Dandekar, V.M. (1994), *The Indian Economy 1947-92*, Vol. 1., Sage Publication.

Dantwala, M.L. *Economic Development and the Role of the Agricultural Sector in India.*

Darling Sir, Malcolm (1955), All India Rural Credit Survey in *International Cooperative Alliance Review,* June, 1955.

Desai, B.M. (1986), "Whither Rural Financial Institution?" *Economic and Political Weekly,* Mumbai.

Desai, D.K. (1990), 'Institutional Credit Requirements for the Agriculture System in India-2000', in *Agricultural Development Policy – Adjustments and Reorientation*, Oxford and IB Publishing, New Delhi.

Dhavan, Narayan, *Agricultural Change and Rural Poverty: Variations on a Theme.*

Fay, C.R., *Cooperation at Home and Abroad,* London.

F.A.O., *New Approach to Agricultural Credit*, 1964.

——, *Agricultural Credit through Cooperatives and other Institutions*, Rome, 1963.

Gadgil, D.R., (1960), 'Towards a Cooperative Commonwealth Professor Brij Narayan Memorial Lectures,' University of Punjab.

Gadgil, M.V. (1994), 'Formal Agricultural Credit System in India, Shape of Things to Come' *Indian Journal of Agricultural Economics*, Vol. 49, No, 3, July – September.

Government of India (1996), Concurrent Evaluation of Integrated Rural Development programme (IRDP) – A Report, *Government of India*, October, New Delhi.

——, (1996a), 'Report of the Working Group on Agricultural Credit and Co-operation (Including Crop Insurance) for the Formulation of Ninth Five-Year Plan', *Government of India*, August, New Delhi.

——, *Economic Survey* (1997-98), 1998-99.

Hough, E.A., *Co-operative Movement in India.*

Islam, Rizwaul, *Strategies for Alleviating Poverty in Rural India.*

Jain, S.C., *Management in Agricultural Finance*. Vora, Bombay, 1970.

Karve, D.G. *Rural Development.*

Kaladhar, K. (1996), 'Designing Financial Services for Rural Poor—Retooling Rural Financial Institutons', *Economic and Political Weekly*, September 28.

——, (1997), 'Competitive Rural Financial Markets' *CAB Calling*. January-March.

——, (1995), 'Self-help Groups—The Next Stage' — *CAB Calling*, Vol. 18, Nos, 3 & 4; July - September.

Ketkar, K. (1993), 'Public Sector Baking Efficiency and Economic Growth in India—*World Development*, Vol. 21 (10), October 1985 –97.

Khawa, Ashok, L. Adkins and S. Meyanathan (1992) "Financial Infrastructure, Issues for Developing Countries"—*Economic Development Institute* (EDI) Working papers, The World Bank.

Kohli, R. (1996), "Replacing Market with Governemnt, The Indian Exerience in Credit Allocation" (Unpublished. Phil. Thesis,University of Sussex, Brighton, U.K.)

——, (1997), 'Directed Credit and Financial Reporm', *Economic and Political Weekly*, No. 42, 1997.

Krishnaswami, K.S., K. Krishnamurthy and P.D. Sharma, (1987), 'Improving Domestic Resource Mobilisation through Financial Development; India', *Asian Development Bank*, Manila.

Louis, P. Smith, *The Evolution of Agriculture Co-operatives*

Mathur, D.P., *Public Sector Banks in India's Economy*

Ministry of Agriculture (1971), Interim Report of the National Commission on Agriculture on Credit Services for Small and Marginal Farmers and Agricultural labourers, December, *Government of India*, New Delhi.

Ministry of Agriculture and Irrigation (1976), "Report of the National Commission on Agriculture', January, *Government of India*, New Delhi.

Morris, F. (1985), 'The Indian Financial System: An overview', *World Bank Discussion Paper*, No. 727.

Majumdar, N.A. (1997), 'The Interest Rate Imbroglis', *The Journal of Indian Institute of Bankers* – July September.

——, (1994), 'Refocussing on Rural Credit, The Macro Dimensions' *Economic and Political Weekly*, October 15.

——, (1995), 'New Banking Culture and the Small Borrowar', *Economic and Political Weekly*, September, 2.

——, (1996), 'Financial Sector Reforms, An Exercise in Introspection' – *Economic and Political Weekly*, September 12.

——, (1996-97), 'Development Imperatives and the Banking System'- *Prajnan*, Vol. XXV, No. 53-54.

——, (1997), 'Overhauling the Somnobut Rural Credit System' *Economic and Potential Weekly* No. 42, 1997.

——, (1998), 'Credit Support to Priority Sectors' – *A Macro Perspective – Economic and Political Weekly*, No. 4, 1998.

NABARD (1994), 'National Seminar on Rural Credit' held on September 1 in Mumbai, *Background Papers*.

——, (1994), 'Report of the Study Group on the Rural Non-Farm Sector' –*National Bank for Agriculture and Rural Development*, Mumbai.

——, (1997, 1998), *Annual Reports*, 1997-98, Mumbai,

——, (1998b), 'Review of Working of Regional Rural Banks', *National Bank for Agriculture and Rural Development*, Mumbai,

Pal, Arindam (1997), 'Rural Credit: An Overview'—Paper Presented in National Seminar on Management of overdues in Rural Banking held between Agre 10-11 at Tirupati, Andhra Pradesh.

Palit, Urjit, R. (1997), 'Emerging Reforms in Indian Banking, International Perspectives', *Economic and Political Weekly*, October.

Planning Commission, Government of India, (1951), 'The First Five Year Plan—A Draft Outline,' July, *Government of India*, New Delhi.

——,(1953), *The First-Five Year Plan*, 1951-56.

Planning Commission, Government of India, (1956), *The Second Five-Year Plan.*

——, (1957), Report on Certain Aspects of Co-operative Movement in India by Sri Malcolm Darling, June, *Government of India.*

——, (1962), *Third Five-Year Plan 1961-66.*

——, (1969), *Fourth Five-Year Plan (1969-74).*

——, (1980), *India' Sixth Five-Year Plan 1980-85.*

——, (1985), *Seventh Five-Year Plan 1985-90,* Vols. I & II, Govt. of India, New Delhi.

——, (1992), *Eighth Five-Year Plan (1992-97),* Vols. I & II.

——, (1997), *Approach Paper to the Ninth Five-Year Plan.* (1997-2002), Government of India, 1996.

Puhazhendhi, V. (1995), 'Transaction costs of lending to the poor, Non-Governmental Organisations and Self-help Groups of the poor as Intermediaries for Banks in India', *Foundation for Development Cooperation.* Brisbane, Australia.

——, (1996), 'Viability of Service Functions by cooperatives; An Imperical Analysis' *Indian Journal of Agricultural Economics,* 51 (4), October –December.

Rao, Ch. Hanumantha (1998), 'Agricultural Growth, Sustainability and Poverty Alleviation—Recent Trends and Major Issues of Reform', *Economic and Political Weekly,* July 18.

Reserve Bank of India (1954), *All-India Rural Credit Survey Report of the Committee of Direction,* Vol. II-general Report (Chairman A.D. Gorwala) – RBI, Bombay.

——, (1962), *All India Rural Debt and Investment Survey* 1961-62.

——, (1964), Report of the Informal Group on Institutional Agreements for Agricultural Credit, December (Chairman P.C. Bhattacharya), RBI, Bombay.

——, (1969), *Report of the All-India Rural Credit Review Committee,* 1969.

Reserve Bank of India, (1971-72), *All India Rural Debt and Investment Survey 1971-72, 1981-82 and RBI*, Bombay.

——, (1972), *Report of the Banking Commission.*

——, *Rural Credit Follow-up Survey 1956-57.*

——, *Studies in Agricultural Credit.*

——, (1974), *Report of the Study Team on Overdues of the Cooperative Credit Institutions*, February (Chairman C.D. Daley), -RBI.

——, (1978), *Report of the Committee to study the Functioning of Public Sector Banks* (Raj Committee) 1978.

——, (1978), *Report of the Export Group on Agriculture Credit Schemes of Commercial Banks* (Desai Committee), 1978.

——, (1979), Report of the Committee for Reviewing Arrangements for Financing Institutional Credit for Agriculture and Rural Development (CRAFICARD); Interim Report, November, Report, March 1981 (Chairman B. Sivaraman), RBI.

——, (1979), *Regional Rural Banks*, Report of the Review Committee (Dantwala Committee), Nov. 1978.

——, (1980), *Report of the Working Group on Priority Sector Lending and the 20 Point Programme—Role of. Banks* (Chairman K.S. Krishnawami), April, 1980.

——, (1984), *Report of the Working Groupon the Role of Banks in Implementation of New 20-Point Programme* (Chairman A. Ghose), RBI 1984.

——, (1985), *Report of the Committee to Review the Working of the Monetary System* (Chairman — Dr. Sukhomoy Chakravorty), Bombay 1985.

——, (1987), *Report of the Working Group on Money Market* (Chairman N-Vaghel), Bombay, 1987.

——, (1991), *Report of the Committee on the Financial System*, November (Chairman — M. Narasimham).

Reserve Bank of India, (1998), *Report of the Narasimham Committee* (2nd Report), April 23, 1998.

(1998), *Report of the High-Level Committee on Agricultural Credit through Commercial Banks* (Chairman R.V. Gupta), RBI, Bombay.

——, (1998), *Report of the Working Group on Rural Credit Planning and Monetoring by Banks*; (Charman P.V.A. Rama Rao), 1998.

Roy Durgadas, *Agricultural Co-operations and Economic Development, The Indian Perspective:* Nalanda Publications Private Ltd., Calcutta 1989.

——, *Consumer Cooperatives in India with Special Reference to West Bengal—An Analysis of its Growth and Development*, Rabindra Bharati University, Calcutta, 1992.

Rudra, Ashoke, (1990), 'Co-operatives— The Forgotten Alternative' in *Agricultural Development Policy—Adjustments and Reorientation*, Oxford and IBH Publishign, New Delhi.

Satish, P. and C.K. Gopalkrishna (1977), 'Viability of Rural Banking', *Economic and Political Weekly*, Vol, 32, No. 42.

Satyasai, K.J.S., and K.U.Viswanathan (1996a), 'Commercialisation and diversification of Indian Agriculture', *Economic and Political Weekly*, Nov. 9-16.

Shah, Tushaar, (1995), 'Liberalisation and Indian Agriculture, New Relevance of Farmer Cooperative'-*Indian Journal of Agriculture Economics*, 50(3), July-September,

Shukla, Tara, *Economics of Underdeveloped Agriculture*, Vora, Bombay, 1969.

Singh, S.P. and Mrityunjaya (1992), Impact of short term Credit on Income and Employment of Marginal and Small Farmers', *Agricultural Economics Research Review*, Vol. 5, No. 1.

Tokhi, M.N., & B.P. Sharma, *Rural Banking in India.*

Viswanathan, K.U., K.J.S. Satyasi and V. Puhazhendhi, (1995), 'Liberalisation in Agricultural Sector: Implications for Rural

Credit and Small Farmers', *Indian Journal of Agricultural Economics*, 50(4), July-September.

Von Pischke, J.D, (1980, "The Pitfalls of Specialised Farm Credit Institutions", *Development Digest*, Volume 18, No, 3, July, pp. 79-91.

World Bank, (1995), 'Report on Financial Services for Rural Poor and Women in India', *Access and Sustainability*, New Delhi, March.

Yaron, Jacob (1992), 'Successful Rural Finance Institutions', *World Bank Discussion Paper*, No. 150.

Index

F

G

H

I

J

K

L

M

N